IN SEASON
OUT OF SEASON

An Introduction to the Thought of Jacques Ellul

Translated by Lani K. Niles

Based on Interviews by Madeleine Garrigou-Lagrange

1817

HARPER & ROW, PUBLISHERS, SAN FRANCISCO
Cambridge, Hagerstown, New York, Philadelphia
London, Mexico City, São Paulo, Sydney

FIRST U.S. EDITION

Designed by Donna Davis

Library of Congress Cataloging in Publication Data

Ellul, Jacques.

    IN SEASON, OUT OF SEASON

    Translation of: A temps et à contretemps.
    1. Theology—Addresses, essays, lectures.
    I. Garrigou-Lagrange, Madeleine. II. Title.
BR85.E4914   1982   230'.42'0924   82-47743
ISBN 0-06-062239-3

82 83 84 85 86 10 9 8 7 6 5 4 3 2 1

Contents

Introduction to the American Edition

It is more than a little ironic that Aldous Huxley was one of the key figures in unleashing the flood of Ellulian "prophecy" into America over the past twenty years. Huxley, who admired but could not share Ellul's Christian faith, was deeply impressed by Jacques Ellul's *La Technique, ou l'enjeu du siècle*, which appeared in 1954. In conversations with John Wilkinson, Robert Hutchins, and others at the Center for the Study of Democratic Institutions in Santa Barbara in 1959–1960, Huxley said that Ellul's work was comparable in importance to Spengler's *Decline of the West* and that it "made the case" he had tried to make in *Brave New World*. As a result of Huxley's enthusiasm, discussion groups were organized around Ellul's book. New York publisher Alfred Knopf commissioned John Wilkinson to prepare a translation, which appeared in 1964 as *The Technological Society*.

Although two smaller books by Jacques Ellul had appeared in America earlier (*The Presence of the Kingdom*, 1951, and *The Theological Foundation of Law*, 1960), it was *The Technological Society* that created the first major stir of interest. It was reviewed widely, adopted as a textbook in many college classes, and generated both heat and light in various discussions of contemporary life in America. Typical of the intellectual response to Ellul were the comments of Theodore Roszak and Alvin Toffler. Roszak, in *The Making of a Counter Culture*, found Ellul "far too verbose and crushingly pessimistic" but nevertheless offering "the best theoretical statement" on the technocracy. Toffler reported in *Future Shock* that Ellul's books were "enjoying a campus vogue" but rejected Ellul as an extreme "future-hater" and "technophobe."

Knopf followed up the growing interest in Ellul's sociological analysis by publishing *Propaganda: The Formation of Men's Attitudes* in 1965, *The Political Illusion* in 1967, *A Critique of the New Commonplaces* the following year, and *Autopsy of Revolution* in 1971. While the technological optimists and the statistical sociologists cringed at both the methods and conclusions of his work, Ellul had become a social analyst to be reckoned with in America. Voices such as Herbert Marcuse, Marshall McLuhan, E. F. Schumacher, and John Kenneth Galbraith, while they differed with him at various points, echoed Ellul's analysis of modern technology and politics.

Many Americans became aware of Ellul's sociological analysis without realizing that he was producing a parallel stream of theological and ethical books. His theological orientation was intentionally "bracketed out" of his major sociological studies. Alvin Toffler mislabelled Ellul a "French religious mystic." Paul Pickrel's cover note on the paperback *The Technological Society* misrepresented Ellul as a "Catholic." (He is in the Reformed Church of France.) Ellul has not trumpeted his Christianity in his sociological works for several reasons. First, he wants his sociological analyses to be validated by brute facts and ordinary experiences and observations, without requiring an advance faith commitment. Second, his writings flow from a career characterized by two more or less separable tracks. On the one hand he is a professor of history and sociology at a state university of a very secularized nation. On the other hand he is an active preacher, churchman, and lay theologian. The sociological writings, even more than the theological writings, flow from what is deliberately not an "integrative" position. Third, Ellul believes that most progress in understanding will come from a dialectical confrontation of a realistic sociology on the one hand, with a revelational theology on the other. In his view, attempts to resolve this dialectic in an intellectual synthesis have been premature and misguided. Thus it has been possible for people to hear only the sociologist without meeting the theologian.

Among the early promoters of Ellul's theological and ethical importance, Episcopalian lay theologian William Stringfellow has special importance. In *The Theological Foundation of Law,* he found Ellul to be a kindred spirit. Stringfellow wrote in his introduction to the Seabury Press edition of *The Presence of the Kingdom* that Ellul's work was "authentically prophetic." Seabury Press followed with another half-dozen of Ellul's theological and ethical books during the 1970s. The Christian Reformed publisher William B. Eerdmans got into the act with *The Meaning of the City* in 1970 and followed that with several other biblical and theological studies by Ellul.

Other voices as well were asking for a hearing for Ellul's theological thought. In 1970 Will Campbell and

James Holloway, the prime movers in the Committee of Southern Churchmen, devoted a special issue of their journal *Katallagete* to a series of articles on the meaning and importance of Jacques Ellul. This series was then published in book form as *Introducing Jacques Ellul*. The Committee of Southern Churchmen was a fellowship of southern clergy who mounted a witness aimed at liberating not only the oppressed (in this case, southern blacks), but also the oppressors (e.g., the Ku Klux Klan), a two-edged sword often wielded by Ellul himself. *Katallagete* has continued to run frequent articles by and about Ellul.

An amazingly diverse group of Christian leaders has affirmed the importance of Jacques Ellul's work over the past dozen years. Church of the Brethren theologian Vernard Eller has published several important articles and reviews on Ellul in the *Christian Century*, *Katallagete*, and elsewhere. Lutheran Martin Marty called Ellul the "Protestant voice for our time." Mennonite John Howard Yoder sees Ellul's approach to Christ and power as perhaps one that is "most consistently within" Yoder's own stance in *The Politics of Jesus*. Os Guinness lauded Ellul as the "critical voice of the seventies" in his *Dust of Death*. Yale Old Testament scholar Brevard Childs commended Ellul's biblical exposition as a "highly creative, robust theological interpretation which cannot but stimulate serious reflection." Jim Wallis, of *Sojourners*, and many other "young evangelicals" have been heavily influenced by Ellul.

Of course, an equally impressive list of critics of Ellul could also be presented. What is interesting and unusual is the way Ellul's influence has cut across various traditional denominational lines, age groups, and theological orientations. Ellul has had both supporters and critics in evangelical as well as liberal camps, in Reformed as well as Anabaptist circles. When this theological diffusion of influence is added to the sociological impact on various fields such as political science, sociology, law, communications, and history, the result is impressive indeed. Few intellectuals have had such a broad-ranging importance in twentieth-century America.

While the label "prophet" is tossed about rather loosely these days, I believe that in the case of Jacques Ellul it is fully appropriate. The value of the prophet lies in his ability to disturb the status quo, to put in question what is taken for granted, to shed new light on old issues, to bring in a new perspective. As in the commission to the prophet Jeremiah, the prophet acts by "uprooting, tearing down, destroying, and overthrowing," and by "building and planting." The prophet is both angry and compassionate. He brings a Word from outside. He brings a challenge.

On the other hand, the prophet has limitations. The prophet is not a teacher in the full sense of the term. The teacher gives a more complete, reasoned exposition of the truth, filling it out and applying it. Ellul's work has many rough edges and not a few blind spots, overstatements, and contradictions. As "teaching," Ellul's work is lacking in various ways. But as "prophecy," it is an explosive challenge that is ignored only at great loss. Americans need to give a continued and expanded hearing to the Bordeaux prophet in our technological wilderness.

To social analysts, Ellul puts the challenge of Technique:

If Technique is not the most important phenomenon of our era, what is? Are we being misled by surface events so that we are blind to the deeper maincurrents that are the more important forces in the shaping of our existence? Is the growth of the technical, bureaucratic nation-state the answer or the problem?

To social activists, Ellul puts the challenge of revolution and social change: Is ordinary politics effective in bringing about real changes in human life, or is it an illusory activity that strengthens the chains that bind us? Are Third World nations gaining liberation by throwing out the colonial oppressors only to install Western technical, bureaucratic state mechanisms? Is violence ever productive of anything more than further violence?

To those on the political left, Ellul directs especially pointed criticism: Has the left betrayed its commitment to the truly poor, to human rights, to individual freedom? Is the growth of the State desirable? But to those on the political right, Ellul puts the challenge of the power of corporate Technique: If the nation-state is in need of resistance, and if its powers must be scaled down in favor of human freedom, who will then resist the unopposed power of the big corporations? Is not big business as much an impediment to individual freedom as big government?

To all Christians, Ellul puts the challenge of discipleship: In what way are Christians the "salt of the earth" or the "light of the world" today? Are we routinely conformed to the world? Has Technique invaded the church? Are we mediating freedom and hope in our world? Are we bringing a kingdom presence into the world?

To the ecumenical liberal or "mainstream" Christian, Ellul challenges the "critical dissection" of the biblical text and the suppression of the revelation of the Wholly Other God. Are we going beyond the permissible and raising the serpent's question, "Yea, hath God said?" Are we buying into modernity at the cost of the Christian soul, simply blessing and baptizing opinions arrived at by extra-biblical, often technical, means? Has the Spirit of God departed from our church?

To the evangelical, Ellul poses similarly challenging questions: Are we imprisoned by a wooden, proof-texting view of Scripture that takes account of neither the historical situation of the original revelation nor its place in the canon as a whole? Are we neglecting public discipleship in favor of an exclusive concern for the inner-life and after-life? Are we preoccupied with intellectual doctrine at the expense of the Christian life itself?

Of course, as Ellul raises these challenges, his style is not that of a gentle armchair intellectual eager for a fascinating conversation. There is usually a charge rather than a question. Sometimes Ellul hits a few innocent targets in his prophetic fury and iconoclasm. But he is right more often than we would like, and even when wrong his accusations are healthy challenges that can force a helpful exercise in self-criticism.

Finally, Ellul provokes a kind of dialogue, for he is not immune from our questions either. Has he overstated the case for Technique and the nation-state? Can everything be subordinated to the overarching rubric of Technique? Is there not something extremely important and life-changing occurring with decolonization, even if Western Technique is imported? Don't electoral political decisions sometimes have decisive effects on our life, even if government bureaus do make most of the day-to-day decisions? Is it necessary to engage in a typological reading of the Bible to force it into a kind of canonical harmony? Is it necessary to opt for a final "universalism" rather than to maintain some version of heaven and hell as decisions open to free individuals?

Again, if Ellul were pretending to construct a comprehensive theology on the order of Karl Barth's *Church Dogmatics* we might well take him to task. Read as prophecy, however, Ellul's challenges are well-timed and well-placed. If we cannot accept his view, well and good; let's do it differently, but let's do it better. It is not necessary to be a universalist or a typological expositor of Scripture to profit immensely from Ellul's writing. And it is not necessary to become an anarchist and refuse to vote to profit from his sociological and political writings.

Discussion of Ellul's thought is bound to continue; he has numerous books in print and more on the way. For students of Jacques Ellul's work, *In Season, Out of Season* will assume singular importance. Its uniqueness lies first of all in the fact that it gives a broad and unified introduction to the whole Ellul corpus. Not many people will have the time or the temperament to read all of Ellul's writings, but it is a fact that Ellul is best, if not only, understood after one has consumed a dozen or so of his key works. For the person encountering Ellul for the first time, or for the one who seeks clarification after reading several of his works, *In Season, Out of Season* will provide some essential light on the thought that pervades his books.

Second, but equally important, *In Season, Out of Season* provides the best and most complete biographical information on Jacques Ellul. Ellul has often pointed out that his ideas and analyses are rooted in his own experience. His political analysis must be understood in light of his term in the Bordeaux mayor's office and his work in the Resistance. His stance toward the church must be understood in light of his church experiences. His view of Marxist-Christian thought must be seen in relation to his own Marxist and Christian experience. And so on. Many things in Ellul's work make much better sense after reading his story. It hardly needs to be added that this is even more true given the differences between French and American life.

In Season, Out of Season is a window into the life and heart of one of our century's finest prophetic voices. "The voice of one crying in the wilderness, Prepare ye the way of the Lord."

DAVID W. GILL

New College Berkeley
Berkeley, California

Prologue

It isn't easy to find an open spot on Jacques Ellul's calendar. It is even harder to find four or five hours free in the space of one week. But when they are duly noted on his calendar between two other hourly allotments, each precisely measured, these intervals of time are offered unreservedly.

This generosity in what he first measured so parsimoniously is only one more paradox in the personality of Jacques Ellul. Scholar and activist, sometime pastor, and prolific author of two series of works that, for nearly forty years, have progressed in parallel, he occupies, wherever he is, a place that anyone else would find uncomfortable; yet it is the only place where he can feel perfectly at ease.

Is he right-wing? Left-wing? Everyone ends up confused when they try to assign him a fixed position. He doesn't mind exasperating those who demand a label. He irritates, he unsettles people. He can generate enthusiasm, too. But if he is a prophet, he is honored more in the New World than in the Old. Yet for that matter, anyone who took the same path as he would undoubtedly have had exactly the same results. This man knows the power of his own words to gain a following, and he fears more than anything to be blindly followed. A fighter, he could have made a career of it, carrying into intellectual battle the arms of demagogy. Nothing would have been more repulsive to him.

— M. G.-L.

1.

The Gospel and *Das Kapital*

MADELEINE GARRIGOU-LAGRANGE: *For more than thirty years the plan for your books has existed in your mind, fully developed. And your days seem just as strictly programmed as your life's work. To begin with, would you say that your childhood determined the man you have become?*

JACQUES ELLUL: I really don't have that impression. At the age of eighteen, I had a fairly wide panorama of possibilities, and my life was to be shaped rather by a series of separations and coincidences. You might say that is characteristic of me: though coincidences have started me in certain directions (the Resistance, for example), in other respects, when I have had the impression that I was being caught up in the system, I have tried to disengage myself. The number of radical breaks I have made is significant, I think. I served as a consultant on certain special committees of the Ecumenical Council, and I left voluntarily. I was for twenty years a member of the national council of the Reformed Church of France, and I left voluntarily. These breaks did not result from a change of mind or from instability, but from a sort of judgment that was both realistic and spiritual. I made some sudden reversals. For example, not long after the liberation, I took up the defense of collaborators who were imprisoned in the camps of Eysses and Mauzac because they were being treated as the resistants had been treated by the Nazis during the war. I couldn't tolerate that. I sometimes judged the Resistance severely because of the profits that many made from it. Too, I decided on these breaks whenever I had the impression that I was being conditioned by the group or by the milieu, whenever things became a kind of routine.

Even with all these breaks, your life has still been ordered according to some fundamental choices, those of Marx and Jesus, hasn't it?

Yes, choices that explain in retrospect all the rest, of course. But it is fairly typical that I have never been orthodox anywhere. For example, I always remained on the fringes of the Reformed Church, even while serving on the national council; this is characteristic of my refusal of easy intellectual or institutional orthodoxy. I have never embraced an orthodox theological position. And I have not been any more willing to listen to a ready-made Marxism. I reread Marx from my own perspective, and moreover, I felt no need to communicate it to others. Nothing seems more useless to me than to consecrate my efforts to a "new interpretation of so-and-so." Basically—and perhaps most significantly—every time I have acquired a belief, in any domain, the first thing I have done is to conduct a criticism of this belief. I remember when Christianity, or rather Jesus Christ, imposed himself upon me. I immediately read the works of Celsus[1] and the Baron d' Holbach. In other words, I looked for the strongest evidence against it, asking myself, "Will this hold up, or will I permit myself to be convinced by the contradictors of Christianity, whether they be as ancient as Celsus or from the eighteenth century, like d' Holbach? And, well, it held up in spite of all the objections.

This is standard procedure for me. When I meet someone with whom I am in instant agreement, I start by searching for points of disagreement.

You have gone through successive conversions. Do you, however, have any beliefs that go back to the early days of your life?

Yes, I do. I recall a passage from the Bible I read as a child. There was a Bible in the house. Some verses struck me; one, especially, came back to me recently. I was around ten or eleven years old at the time; I was

---

1. Platonist and polemical writer of the second century.—TRANS.

reading the Gospels when a sentence leaped out at me: "I will make you fishers of men." This phrase haunted me for years before I had any idea what it could mean. Why? Why does a phrase become true? I don't believe that it corresponded to some unconscious desire.

And it doesn't happen only with phrases from the Bible. I have sometimes been captivated by a line of poetry or by an expression from a novel. There is a mysterious instant. Suddenly a phrase becomes a personal utterance. It penetrates into your life. No one knows why, unless it is that, as I've experienced sometimes, you discover ten or twenty years later that this utterance was for you, and it foretold an event. You'd almost think it was "fated to happen," which I don't believe in at all. At any rate, *one* phrase of the Gospels had deeply penetrated into me long before I understood anything at all or even considered the question of God's existence.

Later, but in another way, Marx caused a very profound response in me at the time of the stock market crash of 1929, because my father was out of work and I couldn't understand the injustice that was being done to him. When I came by chance upon *Das Kapital,* I had the sudden impression of a connection. Here and there I uncover these underlying factors that are the source of all I experienced afterward.

Factors that are perhaps explained by your background?

Yes. And I will tell you two or three things that could be significant. First, through my parents, I am a specimen of what people call a *métèque,*[2] a product of the melting

---

2. Derogatory term for a dark-skinned foreigner. —TRANS.

pot. My father had an Italian father and a Serbian mother who was directly descended from the Obreno- viches.[3] And the name Ellul is Jewish; it is the name of a month in the Hebrew calendar. On my mother's side (her maiden name was Mendès, and she may also have had Jewish ancestors), there was a mixture of Portu- guese and French. I am thus a typical foreigner born by chance in Bordeaux, where my parents, also by chance, had settled down. This could explain, if one accepts this sort of explanation, why I have never felt nationalistic. I love France very much, but I have roots everywhere. I feel just as much at home in Italy as in France, and I have strong Serbian roots.

Another factor that explains much: the families of my parents are families that had been rich and became poor. My paternal grandfather was a shipowner at Trieste. He went bankrupt, and following the code of honor of his day, he committed suicide. My father always held him up to me as an example: "This is what an honorable man is like." My grandmother was still young when my grandfather went bankrupt and killed himself. She dressed in black, shut herself up in an apartment, and never left it again.

My mother's family, too, was fairly rich before going broke. We are talking about a circumstance that deeply affected my childhood. Even though my parents were poor (not to the point of abject poverty, of course), they considered themselves a part of the upper bour- geoisie, and they raised me in the traditional values of the

---

3. Serbian dynasty founded in 1817. —TRANS.

conservatives: honor; blameless living; pride in never giving in to pressure; arrogance, no doubt; reaction against all authority; individualism.

Aristocratic values?

Absolutely. We were quite short of money, but we had such a sense of dignity that we would not have asked anyone for help for anything in the world, and at all costs we tried to hide our difficulties from the outside world.

I'll tell you about an event that had a great effect on my childhood. My father had a gift for languages—a gift that I don't have—and he spoke five languages fluently. He was a senior executive in a very large commercial company whose director was an extremely overbearing and quick-tempered man. It was an excellent position for my father. One day, the boss became terribly angry at my father in front of strangers. My father stood up and said to him, "Now you will apologize to me." The boss replied, "If you demand an apology, I'll fire you." "That is pefectly all right with me," said my father, "but I demand an apology." And he was fired. That is when the hard times began, because he had a horrible time finding another job.

Did he remain unemployed?

He had another job after that, but the business went bankrupt in 1922, and he was unemployed again before going through the terrible depression that 1929 brought.

It was a life of uncertainty, with good years and bad years?

There were never any good years. I know that from the time that I was aware of it—ten or twelve years old—there were none. All of my childhood I lived the life you read of in novels about working-class families in the depression.

Did that cause you to have an unhappy childhood?

Not at all. I was perfectly happy. I have wonderful memories of my childhood. Every facet of it brought me happiness: the ice and snow, spring flowers in the public park, the quays and docks that I knew inside and out; the arrivals of transatlantic steamers and the departures of cod-fishing boats; the storms (I loved to go to the park when there was a storm). At home, my playmate was a marvelous cat. Everything was an opportunity for happiness. I didn't need toys. And though I was an only child, I never suffered from loneliness (I enjoyed the silence and solitude) nor from lack of conversation. Nor was I spoiled by my parents as an only child, because they worked away from home too much to be able to shower me with attention. Only one bad memory: the harassment in high school because I was the smallest in the class—and the best student. They made me pay for it at play time!

Were your parents as happy as you were, or were they worried, unhappy?

My father placed such a premium on honor that difficulties didn't affect him. For Mama, it wasn't honor that she valued the most, it was art. She taught painting. I was brought up in an extraordinarily cultured environment in this respect. At fifteen, I can say that I had a true passion for art. Mama had taught me everything, but I was more attracted by the history of art —understanding the great painters—than by the creation of art through my own efforts. This was a reaction that is deeply rooted in my character: I didn't want to paint because my mother painted so well; in the same way, I didn't want to learn languages because my father spoke them so well. Out of pride, no doubt.

Thus I lived in this universe of honor and art that today would be labeled a fantasy world. That doesn't stop me from having memories of an amazingly happy childhood. My parents loved me; that was more important than having toys. Furthermore, I was free, and I had an intense life with my friends. Poverty was a part of everyday life. It had an unusual setting in our case: as in all families that were formerly rich and had lost their fortunes, there was little to eat, but we had a beautiful silver service and set of crystal. We lived on the salaries of a minor office employee and a modest painting teacher. When one of the three of us got sick, it was a disaster. And it should be apparent that this ambiguous nature of our family (aristocratic and poor) led to isolation; for example, no one was ever invited to our home. Never a guest at the noon or evening meal. My father looked down on his co-workers at the office, and he had not wanted to keep in touch with his acquaintances from richer days. Besides, he wouldn't have wanted to entertain someone without being liberal and lavish; since that was impossible, there was thus never a visitor. The family was a solitary island. The first time I invited my fiancée to dinner was a real adventure!

But at the age of twelve, thirteen years old, it was not a big problem for me. I had the immensity of the quays for myself. I had all the countryside around Bordeaux where my friends and I went for walks. It is all built up now, but it was beautiful then. Our poverty started to affect me when I became aware of it. When I received my high school diploma, it was necessary for me to go to work. I was sixteen years old. Some very well-intentioned people came to see my mother and told her, "Now that your son has his diploma, we are prepared to give him a job in our business." My mother thanked them but said, "My son will never have the life my husband had. I want him to become something other than an office worker. He will go to college." But since it was still necessary that I earn a living, I gave lessons. It became a regular industry. At the age of eighteen, I gave three or four hours of lessons every day.

What kind of lessons?

Latin, Greek, German, and French. I am still in touch with some of my old students. They were ten years old, I was sixteen. Now that I am seventy, they are sixty-four.

Did that give you a calling to teach?

If not a calling, at least a love for teaching. At sixteen, I found it extraordinary to transmit something that was more than simple knowledge, to awaken a mind. I can say that I did that for several young children. I have a wonderful memory of it, because very quickly there sprang up between me and my students a climate of confidence great enough that we could go past the stage of rote repetitions. They asked me questions about life, and all the rest, that sometimes embarrassed me a lot and made me think—to find an answer for them. That has been the story of my life: I have never ceased working to find answers to the questions I am asked.

But there was another aspect. I had to work four hours a day giving lessons and do all the rest, too. So when my father was really unemployed, for a long period of time, I had moments of depression. I remember my panic one Saturday when a family didn't pay me for the week's lessons, and I said to myself, "There's no more food in the house." At seventeen years old, that leaves an imprint.

I also recall one evening. It was in December of 1930 or 1931, I can't remember anymore. I was a law student, my father was unemployed, everything depended on what I earned, and—would you believe it—my parents fell ill, both of them. Seriously ill. When I saw that I would have to do the shopping and cooking and take care of my parents in addition to my usual activities, I was in the depths of despair.

But it was certainly at that time that I developed the characteristic you have already observed: my obsession with regulating my use of time. Since I had to do everything (and pass my exams), I very quickly organized myself so that I knew exactly how much time I required for each activity, each errand, each reading assignment. I had to become efficient at all costs. I used the Taylor system[4] on myself. In that, too, I was ahead of my age.

---

4. Efficiency methods for factory management developed by Frederick W. Taylor.—TRANS.

Since it was during this time that our political economics professor spoke to us on Marx's thinking and I borrowed *Das Kapital* from the library and started reading it, you can easily see that the effect this reading had on me was not purely due to chance. I was eighteen years old. I discovered a global interpretation of the world, the explanation for this drama of misery and decadence that we had experienced. The excellence of Marx's thinking, in the domain of economic theory, convinced me.

Was this your first faith?

No, it wasn't a faith. Let's say that it was the first breakthrough giving me a general interpretation of the world, my first general education.

At this point I need to refer back to my childhood. Since my father had done all of his studies in German and Italian, we had in the house a great number of classics in these languages, but nothing in French. My mother was interested only in painting. Thus I lived in complete literary ignorance. In class, I was a very good student. I learned everything there was to learn. In history, in literature, I was always first in the class. But obviously many things were lacking in my education, particularly music. My artistic life had been confined to painting; I never heard real music[5] during my entire childhood. It seems evident that that would be totally unimaginable today.

---

5. I mean by this that all I knew of music is what was played at the cinema by local orchestras for the silent films!

But though I knew everything I was taught, I knew nothing outside of it. And since the teaching of literature at that time didn't go past Leconte de Lisle, I arrived at the university having never heard of Zola, or Gide, or Proust, or Claudel. I knew by heart miles of Latin, Greek, and French poetry—classical poetry. But modern poetry did not exist for me. In 1931 I had never heard of Gide. And when I suddenly realized that since 1880, fifty years had passed, I was seized with an intellectual panic, saying to myself that I would never be able to read all of Proust, that I could never absorb all that. And I was overcome by an insatiable appetite for reading.

But what I wanted to show here is that I had a lot of knowledge but no explanations. I had learned what there was to learn (although I don't think I understood much of Racine); I knew the outline of these literary creations, but I had never grasped their relation to my life, to the world in which I lived. In other words, I understood the form of reasoning, but had no idea what it referred to. And in the same way I excelled in history, but it was just a series of unconnected events, there was no key.

How is it that, in this world explained by Marx, Jesus intervened? Did Marx disappoint you?

Not at all. It is rather a case of parallel paths. I can't say the Christian faith was entirely foreign to me. My mother was Protestant. My father, raised in the Greek

Orthodox religion, was a skeptic, a Voltairian (the bust of Voltaire sat enthroned on the mantel—he was the authority), an epicurean (even in practice, at least during his youth when he had a good position), but very liberal. He held that everything was possible, and he thought that on the subject of religion he should not try to influence me, that I would choose when I grew up. He was very good, very energetic, very charming, and very secretive. It seemed to me that there was some sort of agreement between him and my mother that she would never go to church. He didn't forbid that I receive any kind of Christian education, but nothing was done in that direction. From time to time, I remember, a pastor came to the house. My mother received him as one receives a social caller, nothing more. At any rate, it is obvious that there was not a Christian atmosphere, a Christian upbringing, nor even reference to Christian morality in my home. I only recall seeing my mother kneel at times and perform this mysterious act she called prayer, but I had no idea what it meant.

At the age of fourteen, I did have a year of catechism, which I did not find the least bit interesting. No, there was something— The pastor who taught us the catechism had us read a text from Pascal's *Pensées*, and it struck me. (At the same time in school we were studying *Les Provinciales* of which only the reasoning interested me because we quite naturally understood nothing of the crux of the argument.) There again, a phrase became true. Surprisingly, I never found it again exactly as I had remembered having read it. It was a text by Pascal in which he indicts those who try to walk

two different paths: *"Vae ingredientibus in duabus viis."*
Another text which, a posteriori, I can consider prophetic for me. It is the only thing I got out of this
catechism.

And then there was an event in my life that could be
called a conversion and that I don't wish to relate. We
have heard too many conversion stories. . . . I will
mention just two things on this subject. First, it was as
violent as the most violent conversion you have heard
of; second, I started to run for my life from the One who
had revealed himself to me. It wasn't the kind of
positive conversion that pushes you to read the Bible or
go to church. It was the opposite. No, not exactly the
opposite; I realized that God had spoken, but I didn't
want him to have me. I fled. This struggle lasted for ten
years.

An issue between you and God?

An issue between God and me, without an interme-
diary. I didn't talk about it with anyone. You might say I
wanted to remain master of my life, and I had the
impression that in giving in to this pressure from God I
would no longer be the boss. This explains why, when I
discovered Marx and his explanation of the world, I
preferred to follow that route rather than the one of
Christianity.

In fact, Christianity didn't seem to me at all an
explanation of the world. You can't forget that at that
time the main debate among Christians centered on
salvation, that of the individual. It was a purely personal matter. But it was in this area of the personal

question that I found Marx lacking. He could explain to me my situation but not my human condition, my mortal nature, my capacity to suffer or to love, or my relationship with others. Basically, I was not content with Marx's explanation. So, having this option of consulting the Bible, I read it from time to time, at the same time as several other things. Goethe was one of them, in fact the principal one.

And then, at around age twenty-two, a second stage in my conversion came in reading chapter eight of the Epistle to the Romans; it was an awesome experience for me. It is often said that the Epistle to the Romans is the Protestant epistle. It is the chapter where "nature suffers and groans in the pains of childbirth." It gave me a response both on the individual level and on the collective level. I saw a perspective beyond history, one that is definitive.

Those are my two real sources.

At that time did you feel you had to choose between Christianity and Marxism, or were you an early Marxist Christian?

Because I took Marx's thinking very seriously, his emphasis on the uselessness of considering the question of God's existence and his rejection of all dimensions other than economic or political left me with no hope of a reconciliation. Furthermore, I could see no possibility of systematizing Christianity in the economic and political domains. The social theories of the Church seemed antiquated to me, and I found Christian socialism, socialist Christianity (André Philip had a great influence in Protestantism at that time), very superficial, failing to get to the heart of the problem. Besides, was this revelation I had received from God capable of being systematized? Of being generalized? I saw quite well the possibility of communicating piety and prayer on the individual level but nothing beyond that. I thus remained unable to eliminate Marx, unable to eliminate the biblical revelation, and unable to merge the two. For me, it was impossible to put them together. So I began to be torn between the two, and I have remained so all my life. The development of my thinking can be explained starting with this contradiction.

So when you found yourself confronted with the Christ, you had before you the whole range of Christian creeds. What factor caused you to choose the Reformed Church?

It was reading Calvin's *Institutes.* They seemed to correspond to my personal understanding of the Bible, which was pretty straightforward. During the same period, I read Saint Augustine, and found myself very close to his thinking, and a little of Saint Thomas Aquinas, whom I didn't care for at all. But that was due to an intellectual fault I have always had: I am absolutely not a philosopher, so I remained completely closed to Aquinas's thinking, which seemed philosophical to me. I also read Duns Scotus and certain other great theologians of the Middle Ages, whom I found just as uninteresting as Aristotle and Plato.

Didn't Christianity seem to you to be something completely different from a philosophy?

Yes. And since the revelation, thanks to the Bible and chapter eight of the Epistle to the Romans, had given me a response to an existential question, I had little reason to see any benefit in these intellectual constructions.

Did you also dislike systematizing?

Calvin is very systematic, but I found his works to make constant reference to the biblical text. As I came to know Protestant thought better, I moved away from Calvin and moved closer to Kierkegaard and Karl Barth.

At the time of your conversion, didn't Calvin's radicalism suit you the best?

At that time, this radicalism was a part of my existence. Calvin wrote for battle. His theology is extremely closed. For him, there is only one truth; all the rest is error. In other words, pluralism in any form is incompatible with his thinking. And I must say that fit in very well with my temperament: pugnacious, strict, and in search of truth that naturally at that age can only be closed. I was more open to analytical thought like that of Calvin (the Calvinists are going to challenge me on that) than to synthesizing thought like that of Aquinas. I haven't changed much on this point, but I have changed very much on the exclusivity of systematic truth. I have come more and more to consider that we all have a certain interpretation of the same revealed truth, but no one possesses it completely. We all ought to come together in such a way that we each may recognize in others what we lack in ourselves.

Wasn't it uncomfortable for you to reconcile two equally totalitarian truths, that of Calvin and that of Marx? Didn't you feel as if you were being torn in two?

Exactly. And the most uncomfortable part actually was to be in the presence of two such exclusive thinkers, each as totalitarian as the other. I couldn't give up either one of them.

Under these conditions, my thinking could only develop dialectically: either I would stay rooted at the point where I was, torn in two, and would become literally schizophrenic, or I would go past the contradiction by walking, as Mao said, on both legs, being able to respond to an existential situation, to a historical or political one. When I did this, I again encountered the contradiction and I again had to go forward. This expression of Mao's—walking on two legs— referred to something entirely different, but I can't count how many times I have applied it to myself.

For Mao, the legs were following two paths that were pretty much parallel.

In my case, I was able to be intellectually strict with Marx's thinking in the area of world interpretation. Moreover, I was convinced from the beginning that there could be neither Christian politics, nor Christian economics, nor a Christian society, but that the revelation contributes a fundamental existential truth. It was necessary to work it out so that these two truths could be lived together—I do mean lived, not reconciled intellectually in a system. The economic and political facets of Marx's thinking (I knew nothing then of his philosophical thought) became for me a good framework for comprehending the society in which I lived. But the revelation (which I began to distinguish from Christianity because, under the influence of Bernard Charbonneau, I very soon mistrusted all "isms") allowed me to live in society, to be alive in it.

While all this was going on, you studied law at the University of Bordeaux. What made you choose this path?

It was certainly not a calling. All during my years in high school I had only one interest, the sea; only one aim, to become a naval officer. This was the goal toward which I worked. And then, when I graduated from high school, my father told me, "Now, you are going to study law." I went through some rebellion, but when my father said something, there was no question of putting up an argument.

I thought your father was rather liberal.

He was, to the extent that he never held me back in my initiatives. In certain areas, he demanded a strict discipline of me. For example, I had to be at the dinner table on time. But aside from some very precise obligations, I did just about whatever I wanted.

My father was also liberal in the realm of ideas. When I became definitely leftist, he was unmoved; he let me do it, with a certain irony. On the other hand, he had an aristocratic conception of the father of the family. What he said could not be disputed.

He chose your life for you?

Yes, in a sense, but I had such great confidence in him.

And why law?

For a reason that is very easy to understand. My father, who had had to go into the business world very young, had a passion for law, and his only regret was not to have studied it. Since he hadn't been able to do it, I had to. There you have it. My father had spoken, and I accepted, but after a few weeks I affirmed, "Then I will go all the way with it."

You mean, to a professorship?

I didn't know at all then. I was only seventeen. But I didn't want any of the professions that law represented to me: lawyer, judge, bailiff. They were all out of the question for me. I thus engaged in this line of study without taking any interest in it.

And it never interested you?

I quickly developed a love for Roman law because of its imperturbable logic, and because I liked history. Even in high school, nothing excited me so much as history. I was a historian because I liked it, because I was impassioned by it. The rest did not interest me in the least. Since I had a good working intellect, I passed all my exams easily, but I found nothing interesting except Roman law. Later, when I had my degree, I went to my professor of Roman law and told him, "Now I want to prepare for professorship." He replied, "We'll see. I don't know if it is possible. First do a brilliant thesis."

Because there were few teaching positions open at the time?

I should perhaps explain that the *agrégation* in the school of law is not the same as in literature or sciences. In law, one must first obtain the doctoral degree, and the higher degree for professorship is based on a competitive exam that gives access to university teaching posts. This exam is only given every two years, and it gives access only to those posts that have become vacant during those two years. In Roman law, there were from two to five positions for each exam for the entire university system.

So yes, they were few in number. But I worked toward this goal. And when I went through a period of rebellion, I worked with a sort of sarcastic humor. I thought, "Isn't it extraordinary? Here I am going to become a professor of Roman law and be very well paid by a society that I will not be serving in any way. Because it is quite clear that Roman law is of no use to anything or anyone." I was taking a little personal revenge on society; I thought my joke was quite good.

Roman law gave you a purely abstract pleasure?

Not purely abstract, no. On the one hand there was indeed the beauty of reason, a mathematical kind of beauty, to which was added, however, a human substance. Roman law speaks of things that people have lived and invented; it has this historical dimension to it that I liked. And then, I had always enjoyed reading the Latin writers, much more than the Greeks; I felt in harmony with the Roman mind. They were not philosophers, either. Roman law attracted me even by its structure: a pragmatism proceeding by analysis of reality, and then reconstruction of this reality by applying precise categories, finally arriving at the resolution of concrete human problems. It was never a matter of abstract deductions nor even of arbitrary regulations. Moreover, up until the classical period, it was a system of law developed outside of the political powers; it took experience very much into account, to the point that it seemed to me to fulfill the role of a barrier against abuses of power. And certainly, even at that time, I didn't like the state. This took place during the thirties, when fascisms and ideologies of the state sprang up everywhere. We'll talk more of that later.

2.

Fortuitous Friendships

JACQUES ELLUL: It is impossible to go any further in my account without mentioning a biographical fact that has had a very important place in my life: friendship. If I absolutely had to describe myself, I would say that I am a man of friendships. I have had the good fortune to have some of the most astonishing and extraordinary friends.

At the age of fifteen, I was a typical good student, a real intellectual machine. As I remember myself in those days, I was a very open kid, but I didn't have a nickel's worth of human kindness. I was lucky to have had at an early age friends who have enriched my life. And nothing has separated us, even though we have sometimes had some great differences of opinion.

A case in point is when my closest friend during the days of my youthful intellectual crisis decided to go into a career in the army. He went to the military school at Saint Cyr at the moment I became a pacifist, advocate of nonviolence, conscientious objector, and so on. It was traumatic. Thus there was in my life not only the intellectual conflict between Marx and Jesus Christ, there was also the conflict caused by the decision of my best friend (now dead), to become a military officer. Well, our friendship was not lost. I would almost say that, contrary to the famous expression "*Amicus Plato, sed magis amica veritas*," to me a friend is more important than the truth. And doubtless this attitude toward life that I came by quite spontaneously, this top priority, predisposed me to the Christian faith: when I had indeed understood that herein lay the unity of love and truth, that conflict was no longer possible in Jesus, then I recognized truth in the person who manifested God's love. I hadn't come to that yet when I met Pierre. Nevertheless, in later years, an event brought us even closer together: he was an atheist, and during our relationship he was converted. I really cannot say that I converted him. That would be all the less true because he became a Catholic, a very good Catholic. But his conversion brought us closer together, overshadowing our political differences.

A second friend had major importance in my life. He is Bernard Charbonneau, with whom—I'll come back to it later—I joined the movement *Esprit*.[1] He was my

---

1. *Esprit*, which means "mind" or "spirit" in French, was the name

companion through the years in many other battles. We met each other in high school, and we experienced both very close communion of ideas and perpetual confrontation, because he was non-Christian, and even rather violently anti-Christian.

MADELEINE GARRIGOU-LAGRANGE: *He remained that way?*

I believe so. But in a rather remarkable position: I think he all the more violently opposes Christians because he believes more than they in Jesus Christ. I can't say that he believes in the traditional way, but I don't see any other way to describe what he has written about Jesus Christ—which is overwhelming—than as an expression of faith. What he can't tolerate about Christians is that they have betrayed completely, he believes, everything that Jesus brought to the world. Thus, every time we meet I have to listen to an indictment of Christians (and not only of the Church). Only after that can we communicate.

This hasn't prevented you from undertaking a work in collaboration.

No, but he has had some incredibly bad luck. Although I consider him to be one of the greatest writers of his generation, having an admirable style, none of

--,

of a movement (and its journal) often known as personalism. Emmanuel Mounier was the leading thinker in this movement which influenced Dorothy Day, Peter Maurin, and the Catholic Worker Movement in the United States.—TRANS.

his great books has been published. It is true that his thinking is so original that it is hard to enter into his universe. I call it bad luck, but that is not really accurate. In all of his writing, Bernard has been a lucid (the only lucid one of our age) and harsh adversary of modern society as it developed from the aftermath of World War I. And, to use his own explanation, it has been impossible for him to be published and to form a following because when one attacks the heart of the social structure, the social body defends itself at the point of attack; publishing is a social function that defends the social order. The social order includes those who question it (for example, communism, whose challenge confirms the order), but not if they question too far. The fact remains that Bernard Charbonneau, one of the rare geniuses of our time, is completely unknown. He has had a decisive influence in my choice of direction in research and thought; he has in a way triggered all my development. Without him, I think I wouldn't have done very much—at least, I would not have discovered anything.

My third friend was the Reformed Church theologian Jean Bosc. He had a very great influence on me.

When did you meet him?

Later than the others, around age twenty-two or twenty-three. It was he who directed me toward the thinking of Karl Barth, and although I can't say he trained me theologically, I learned much from him in our relationship. He had an amazing personality, one of the rare Christians about whom I have no reservations.

If he had lived in another era and if he had been a
Catholic, I think he would likely have been canonized.

*Isn't he one of the few people you admit had an influence on
you?*

Bernard Charbonneau and Jean Bosc both influenced
me to an extraordinary degree. Without them I wouldn't
exist, it's perfectly evident. To put it another way, two
writings—Marx and the Gospel—and then two people
—Jean Bosc and Bernard Charbonneau—formed my
personality.

Jean Bosc did more than just bring me close to Barth.
He was in our friendship the closest and most truthful
witness of God. We had no secrets between us. Jean was
a Christian of incredible authenticity, and he was to me
the most perfect combination for a model of Christianity that I have ever known. He combined moral rigor
with loving sensitivity, honesty and righteousness with
an understanding of all the weaknesses and all the faults
of others. He had an admirable sense of humor. In my
life, he represented a kind of narrow path, through the
force of his theology and almost more through the
absolute confidence I had in him.

It was comforting to have him beside me, because we
represented two completely different forms of the
Christian faith. On my side, I had always lived it in a
dramatic and fluctuating style, with extreme highs and
lows, knowing every possible doubt and criticism. Jean
was always the same person. I had the feeling that his
faith was unshakable, always there, always open, and
that he didn't experience the spiritual traumas I did. He

held on to the rock of faith, and his whole life radiated from there. I don't know if I had much influence in his life—I didn't have the impression of giving him anything whatsoever—but every time his apartment door opened upon his smile, it was, in my worst moments of distress, like a door opening onto truth and affection. For me, Jean's presence was—yes, I can say it was like the presence of God's love.

My relationship with Bernard Charbonneau was totally different. My friendship with him, though just as close, seemed to have fewer emotional elements. Bernard was very reserved in that way; and on my side, I am seldom demonstrative. Nonetheless, Bernard was the decisive factor in the development of my personality, as he was in my intellectual life. Uncompromising in all domains, he influenced me by his moral standards, his intransigence, and his rigor.

All of my emotional life between the ages of fifteen and twenty-three was centered around these friendships. Women had no part in my life until I met the one who was to become my wife. But I have to clarify that these masculine friendships have nothing whatsoever to do with homosexuality, neither consciously nor unconsciously. I know the theories on unconscious homophilia; they are absurd, based on a pedantic, humbug psychoanalysis. In reality, they on the one hand negate friendship (which has a nature independent of *eros*, and is for that reason nowadays considered suspect), and on the other hand rehabilitate homosexuality, following the popular trend that consists of showing that this deviation is completely normal, that everyone is homosexual, and ergo, friendship ought to

be considered as such. I have had homosexual acquaintances, and I can guarantee that their relationships had nothing in common with the friendships I
have had.

*You applied the same word, "rigor," to Jean Bosc and to
Bernard Charbonneau.*

I would say that, in my circle of friends, I was in a sense
flanked by these two friends who, without being in the
least bit moralists, had the same kind of rigor in the
ethical domain. On one side, the moral stature of Jean,
based on his faith; on the other, the intellectual rigor of
Bernard Charbonneau, his requirement of being constantly authentic, never distorting what must be said or
done. And he applied this requirement to himself as
well as to those around him.

Bernard Charbonneau had another important role in
my personality development. He introduced me to the
world of nature—the mountains, the joys of camping
and hiking. Before I met him, I was thoroughly a city
boy because of the circumstances of my childhood. It
was Bernard who uprooted me from the urban world to
make me encounter an unknown dimension that was to
occupy a large place in my life.

I have already underlined the fact that Bernard
Charbonneau was at the origin of my thinking and my
research. Before knowing him, at around eighteen or
nineteen years old, I was very studious; all I knew came
from books. My encounter with Marx was the most
original thing that had happened to me, and Bernard,
who also had been influenced by Marx, opened my eyes

to a certain number of essential elements in Marx's thinking.

But more important, he also had a sort of tragic apprehension of the world in which we found ourselves, and through his experience he helped me comprehend the nature of our society. In a very concrete way he put me onto the path that would be one of the two great research topics of my lifetime: Technique.[2]

That isn't all. Throughout my life Bernard Charbonneau has held the role of a critical conscience. And it is irreplaceable. Every time I think or do something, I ask myself what Bernard would think of it or what he'd say to me, knowing full well that his criticism would always be unforeseeable and new.

Despite the profound friendship we share, he has never compromised his standards for my sake. I said that he always shows extreme vehemence toward Christians, all the more so because he perfectly understands what Christianity should be, how Christians should live. One reason for his attitude is a sort of hopeless love for this revelation that remains very important to him. Consequently, he never lets me rest. Every time I assert my faith, I come up against someone who shows me the weakness, the uselessness, the emptiness, the uncertainty of this faith. He continually

---

2. "Technique" is the term preferred by Ellul to describe the ensemble of technical knowledge and methods. He prefers it to "technology," based on the etymological meanings, which are the same in English. In other translations, "technology" has been employed, but we prefer to adhere to Ellul's distinction, capitalizing Technique to avoid confusion with the usual denotation of the word. —TRANS.

backs me up against a wall in my identity as a Christian having a certain vision of society and the world but showing myself incapable of harmonizing my own life with my thinking.

Bernard is, then, the critical conscience who accompanies me throughout my life. And when I know he is in disagreement with something I am doing, I feel less assured, since every time he has criticized one of my undertakings, I have had to admit that he was right.

But his self-criticism is so thorough that it succeeds in paralyzing him. He is sometimes incapable of embarking on a project even though it is feasible. I, on the contrary, commit myself to the maximum possible— and then I have to face him, vigilance in the flesh.

Now you can see, I think, what incredible luck I had to have met these two spiritual, intellectual, and compassionate guides who were also my closest friends; they taught me the fullness and the demanding nature of friendship.

I don't undertake my intellectual work solely out of faithfulness to Jesus Christ, but also because of them. They constantly forced me to go beyond the place I was in at a given moment. And even though we see each other rarely now, Bernard remains, even today, this stimulus that keeps me from droning on, repeating, settling down in a life that is self-satisfied.

I haven't yet talked of the most decisive turning point in my life, meeting my wife. But that is too personal an area. I can only talk here about the things I can talk about! There are some things that cannot be expressed; they can be evoked in parable, in metaphor, or in a novel, for example, but not directly. I will just say that meeting her put me on the line where I had to decide whether to accept the faith and my responsibility. Later she carried the hardest load of my life in that she, a spontaneous, unpredictable, imaginative woman, accepted submitting herself to my work discipline. But more than anyone, she has represented (among many other realities) the mirror of my conscience and the demand for truth. She has always kept me from taking myself too seriously. And then I would have to mention the great trials, the great suffering we bore together, but I won't talk about that. I hate exhibitionism. But in this book, one thing bothers me constantly: it is always about *me*, whereas I can't think of myself without her. (And our social context also, of course, gives me a bad conscience in that everything is centered around the masculine, although the hidden feminine is in reality at least as important.)

3.

Entry into Politics

MADELEINE GARRIGOU-LAGRANGE: *Let's go back to the chain of events in your life. You were twenty years old; you were a student. Isn't that the period when you and your friend Charbonneau made your entry into politics?*

JACQUES ELLUL: Both of us, at that time, were very attracted to politics. Bernard, for that matter, was much more advanced than I in knowledge of the social, sociological, and political structures. His criticism of society seemed to me to go further than Marx's, and what I still find extraordinary, he made a global interpretation of society. When today I reread his writings of that period, I am stupefied by their timelessness.

We really have to situate our position in the virulent context of that historical period: the rise of fascisms, Hitler's coming to power, the events of February 6, 1934,[1] the war in Ethiopia; it was difficult not to get caught up in politics. But the hardest was not to give in to a blind commitment to one camp. It would have been so much easier to be a fascist or a communist. But we had to find another political group that would incarnate our beliefs. The Jèze strike at the time of the war in Ethiopia had of course made me firmly antifascist, but one cannot just stand around repeating slogans.

What at that time attracted you to Esprit?

For some time Bernard and I had already been meeting with some friends. We had formed some small groups in the southwest of France. We went on retreats with other young people. And we looked for a home for our revolutionary yearnings.

The adventure of *Esprit* took place in this setting. We both went to a meeting of *Esprit* in 1934. Bernard was, by the way, extremely skeptical. To begin with, the word *esprit* seemed ambiguous to him, allowing the greatest possible misunderstanding and embracing all sorts of compromise. But we met some people there who had conducted the same criticism of modern society that we had in our little group in the southwest. It was therefore a very important encounter.

----

1. A day of right-wing demonstrations in Paris that culminated in a violent attempt at a coup d'état. —TRANS.

Would you say that you kept a critical distance from Esprit?

Certainly. And all the more so because at about the same time, we met Alexandre Marc, Denis de Rougemont, and their group, *Ordre nouveau* [The New Order]. Bernard and I were between the two positions.

How did they differ from each other?

The two groups were exactly parallel. *Ordre nouveau* could also be described as personalist, but it did not have a Catholic influence or orientation. One met more Protestants than Catholics there. One of the pillars was Denis de Rougemont. And the duo of Robert Aron and Arnaud Dandieu gave direction to the group. Dandieu was a man of exceptional quality who died quite young, twenty-seven or twenty-eight. His first books were published around 1927. A whole team was formed around Aron, Dandieu, Alexandre Marc, and Denis de Rougemont. They founded a journal that was an exact parallel of *Esprit,* although a little more systematic.

Charbonneau and I were torn between the two. We were pretty uncomfortable with the Catholicism of *Esprit,* and we were not very much in agreement with the emphasis on planning in *Ordre nouveau,* for this movement had very concrete ideas (for example, they debated a guaranteed subsistence income, which was a totally new idea at that time). The major positions of *Ordre nouveau* were destructuralization of the national framework and evolution toward a grass-roots federalism. It was the socialism of Proudhon, an anarchist philosophy.[2]

What attracted you to each of the movements?

Ordre nouveau attracted us insofar as it seemed to us to manifest a desire for a more concretely revolutionary action and intervention. But there were only nuances of difference between the two movements. For example, federalism was also advocated by *Esprit,* but as a secondary point, whereas it was one of the foundations of *Ordre nouveau.* On the other hand, the community aspect, essential in *Esprit,* remained secondary in *Ordre nouveau.*

Did you finally make Esprit *your definite choice?*

One factor made us very close to *Esprit:* its spiritual roots. And we were personalists[3] in spite of everything. As a matter of fact, around 1934 Bernard and I wrote an article entitled "Personalism, the Immediate Revolution." And later, in 1936, we drew up a project, before Mounier did, for a personalist manifesto.

---

2. I want to point out that, of course, neither *Esprit* nor *Ordre nouveau* ever took the positions attributed to them by Bernard Henry Lévy in the bizarre findings of his *Idéologie Française.* They never had the slightest trace of fascism from 1933 to 1940, but rather an active and profound antifascism. There was certainly a nationalistic tendency, but it is an absurd mistake to confound nationalism (which I don't believe in) with fascism. B. H. L., in his usual way, has done very superficial research.

3. Philosophy defining the greatest good as the free expression and development of the human personality. —TRANS.

Did you ever think of creating your own movement, given your differences with Esprit?

We never considered anything like that. If we had lived in Paris, perhaps we would have done it. But we were in the southwest, and in France nothing can be created outside of Paris. Nonetheless, we tried to modify the positions of *Esprit* by pushing for a revolutionary movement organized on the local level.

Because you believed at the time that political action could change the course of events?

That was the theme of a great debate with Mounier that went on from 1934 to 1937. It was expressed in these terms: will we establish a movement with members, with groups that will serve as a foundation for and training of an effective revolutionary activity? Or will we restrict ourselves, through the readers of *Esprit*, to a much more intellectual influence, or at the most, an ideological one? Charbonneau and I were determined partisans of local, federated groups; furthermore, we created several of them, and they functioned and produced their own bulletins in which we published several articles. But Mounier was resolutely opposed to them. He bluntly refused this orientation and we broke off with him. If I remember correctly, it was at the end of 1937 or in 1938 that the rupture was consummated over this dilemma: whether to establish a movement having a revolutionary impact or to be nothing but a journal read by intellectuals.

Did this revolutionary movement show signs of beginning in these small groups you mentioned a moment ago?

The starting point, for Charbonneau and for me, was the following: To carry out revolutionary activities, we must leave behind all the existing models, those of the democratic political parties, those of the leagues that had a great influence around 1935, and those of the totalitarian political parties. In other respects, since we began at that point in time to aim for a sort of fundamental cultural revolution, the labor union structure that had already degenerated seemed to us of no use. In any case, the parties, leagues, and unions proposed to transform only a part of the world. We thought it was necessary to carry out both a personal and a collective transformation and that this could only take place in a community setting, that of small groups capable of locally inventing their organization and tactics.

And so you launched into this transformation in creating groups. Were they part of the movement Esprit?

The journal *Esprit* and its counterpart, *Ordre nouveau,* seemed to us to furnish an excellent basis for creating these groups. We envisioned small groups of fifteen to twenty people having the goal of both a personal involvement in a community formed by the group and an explosive thrust toward the outside. We thus tried to get *Esprit* to create such groups, and we traveled around France with this goal. It worked in the southwest where we had a few groups. These grass-roots associations were of fundamental importance to us, first, because they contested the centralization in Paris and second, because they were a place where we could concretely test the validity of the ideas and plans presented in *Esprit* and *Ordre nouveau*. Since they were limited to a small number of members, they could practice a total democracy. And we hoped that they would become a setting for inventiveness, for sociopolitical and even economic innovations; for in reality, a certain number of this kind of group could form a sort of counter-power (neither the word nor the theory existed at that time, even though we already had a very modern vocabulary—I have in front of me a work plan from those days in which the two principal points were "structures" and "the problem of meaning," and we had a precise foresight of their meanings today); they could become alternative organizations. For example, in 1937 we dreamed of an alternative university. But we ran into the opposition of Parisians who absolutely did not want development of concrete actions of this kind. They put all the emphasis on the journal and the intellectual impact it could have in the milieu of professors, that of students, and so on. In reality, they shrank back from putting their ideas into practice.

Several times you've mentioned concrete actions, revolutionary impact. What do you mean by that?

We wanted to instigate a new kind of revolutionary movement that would differ even from the one we had experienced in 1936;[4] we had seen very quickly that that one wasn't revolutionary.

Your revolution would radically transform society?

Yes, radically. We wanted to act on the level of the structural realities of this society, the status of the press, all the centralizations, the advertising, and the industrial system, to give some examples. Of course, we had understood Marx's teaching on revolution, and we thought that socialism was the first stage of a more fundamental revolution, that it was the prerequisite; but nothing would be revolutionary if there were nothing beyond this step, if there were not a transformation of our ways of thinking, of all types of centralizing structures, of our standards of living, and of interpersonal relations. These did not seem to be inevitable results of socialism. We had to want these goals and begin preparing for them at once, especially since the Bolshevik experience in 1935 seemed to us to go against what we thought the revolution should be.

And here is where our experience with Mounier was negative: he was not the least bit interested in what seemed central to us, for example, the primacy of Technique, the technicalizing of everything in society, and also nationalism. We were radical antinationalists; we were for the splitting of countries into political microunits whose union would then have constituted Europe.

----

4. Date when a socialist-communist coalition government was elected into office under the leadership of Léon Blum. —TRANS.

Mounier remained very patriotic, at any rate, if not nationalistic. Now, for us, nationalism and centralization of the state were two of the basic dangers (of which the USSR was a good example) that had to be fought.

Did you think that something was immediately possible?

Not immediately, no. But the youth of those days were no less revolutionary than those of today, and they were ready to mobilize. Our groups did not want either communism or fascism; at the same time they did want democracy to become something other than what it was.

It was a period of extreme political violence. Did your revolutionary project fit into this framework of violence?

It seemed impossible to avoid it. And not counting battles with the police—that was secondary—it is certain that, for a young man already calling himself a Christian, simply thinking about the concrete conditions of revolution posed a huge problem to me. I knew that a revolution could only be made by shedding blood. And that is why I am exasperated every time a revolutionary idealist claims that we will be spared the sacrifice of thousands of people. I can see the two of us again, Charbonneau and me, thinking that a society in the process of dehumanizing people and depersonalizing them (to use the terms of that day) allows no other way out than a radical, revolutionary change of all of its structures, of everything that sustains it. This necessarily implied violent action.

And you accepted it?

Without a doubt, at that time we accepted it. Mounier, however, did not accept it.

Wasn't this problem of violence the cause of your separation?

We never debated it as clearly as that, but it probably counted in Mounier's refusal.

I don't think he would ever have accepted that human beings be sacrificed.

Yes, that's very true. However, I realize now that even though the groups that Charbonneau and I dealt with were not violent, if we had started a revolutionary movement, we would certainly not have been able to control it. Later, after a period in which we believed in the possibility of a violent grass-roots revolution, we went deeper into the question, and we decided that the revolution should take place through small community cells that, as they developed, would transform their surroundings. For years Charbonneau and I devoted ourselves to creating small cells of this nature.

I should add, however, that we were greatly lacking in one important element: an organizer. Neither Charbonneau nor I is an organizer. We were perfectly capable of starting groups, but much less capable of coordinating them and perfecting a systematic and somewhat hierarchical organization. It was all the more difficult because we were partisans of a simple federation of these groups; we have always been—and still are—very anxious to avoid being leaders whom everyone follows, but rather to be those who stimulate the rank-and-file people to take initiatives.

Going back to what you said about your acceptance of violence—during that period, wasn't your interpretation of the Bible influenced by Calvin? The Bible is full of blood, and when God acts he doesn't seem to be very concerned about the number of dead bodies. Didn't this view of the Bible have an influence on you?

It's true that at that time I was captivated by my reading in the prophets. I interpreted them on a rudimentary level. I mean by this that I saw the prophets intervene in a particular society and in a particular history to change the course of events and to instigate some warlike operations. With this perspective, I accepted violence. But it still bothered me a lot because I was at the same time a conscientious objector. There is no chance that I would have gone to jail for it, because I had the luck to be exempted from service, which saved me from a good number of problems. The fact remains that I rejected absolutely any military or nationalistic violence. I was antinationalist, and at that time I could not manage to understand the nationalism of the prophets. I only sensed that there was something else behind it, something not purely political.

What eventually became of all these groups we've been talking about?

It so happens that in 1938 I was named professor at

Strasbourg, which pretty well separated me from them. Then came the war and the almost total destruction of the groups. But in 1944 we started over.

In the meantime were the war years and the occupation. Wasn't there a kind of hiatus between the period we've been talking about and the liberation?

Yes. And I will mention that this interim period was marked by the acquisition of something that has never since left me: a down-to-earth political realism. At the time of the Treaty of Munich, for example, I quite simply evaluated the situation in this way: I wasn't a supporter of the treaty, but contrary to an overwhelming majority of Protestant intellectuals of the day, I wasn't opposed to the treaty, for a purely realistic reason—I saw clearly that the treaty would culminate in giving Hitler free rein and destroying our allies' confidence in us. But I believed that being against the treaty would show a total lack of political realism. So I said (and wrote): "To begin the fight, it is either too late or too early." It was too late because if we wanted to win the war against Hitler, we should have begun it in 1935 when the Germans occupied the Ruhr valley. It was too early because if we really wanted to make war on Hitler, we needed to arm ourselves; we were no longer prepared for a military operation. I was making a concrete evaluation that often influences my writing and is rarely understood. In reality, I don't adhere to a particular position; I limit myself to saying, "If we want this result, here is what we have to do." Now, I still have this attitude, and I still make a realistic evaluation,

much more realistic that that of politicians or intellectuals. I understand very well how this may seem
strange coming from someone who calls himself a
Christian. But I can't act any other way: I analyze
reality outside of my own beliefs. And this results in
countless misunderstandings: people believe that when
I say, "If we want to obtain such-and-such a result, we
must do such-and-such," I am advocating the result in
question. Not at all! I believed then that the opponents
to the Treaty of Munich were idealistic dreamers, full of
good intentions but not understanding that a declara-
tion of war at that moment meant certain defeat because of the disproportion of forces in 1938; a delay was
necessary in order to build up an arms advantage.

In saying that, I was not at all advocating war or an
arms buildup. I was making, as I often do, a sort of
realistic evaluation of events without saying what I
personally would do if I were in power.

Isn't this attitude influenced by the fact that you are a jurist?

Perhaps. But also I have a mind like that—cold and
calculating. If I had been a mathematician, I would
have specialized in algebra. And it isn't just by chance
that in the field of law I was attracted to Roman law.
But I also never cease to dispute the law on behalf of the
living. For example, I challenged all the way the legal
orientation in the *Esprit* movement. I have before me
an article I wrote in 1937 entitled "Critiques" in which
I raised my voice against so-called legal studies (on
democracy, sovereignty, etc.) purporting to be from a
revolutionary point of view.

Yet you seem to await and sometimes even to hope for events that will disturb the natural order—God's irruption into history; revolution; everything that hasn't been programmed.

I've seen plans overturned many times, but that never gives me any pleasure. When I establish schedules for my day or my work, I like them to go as planned. That never happens; I'm constantly being disturbed, but that doesn't make me happy. My logical mind rebels against it. This same logical turn of mind when faced with an observation of reality, actually made me oppose the governments of Daladier, Chautemps, and others. But otherwise you are completely right: I analyze reality, I see its most probable course of development, but that doesn't mean I approve of it; on the contrary, what I see is the interaction of blind forces, nature taking its course, and the human role is precisely that of mastering or preventing this chain of events. This role implies a good deal of revolutionary will and also hope. But the first step in revolution is not enthusiasm, it is realistic analysis.

During the years of the occupation, didn't you make some concrete commitments? How did your cold and calculating mind decide to do that?

In May of 1943, I was convinced that the revolution was a possibility after the war. All the same I didn't wait for that moment; I immediately joined the opposition. I told you at the beginning that my life has often been the result of chance. Here is the best example. I made no choice at all when I joined the Resistance.

I often say that it wasn't out of virtue and patriotism that I joined the Resistance. Nor any more out of a belief that I had to do something. Quite simply, there was no other way for me to act. In July of 1940, the Vichy government fired me from my teaching position.

For what reason?

It was one of the historical footnotes of that period. As I already mentioned, I taught at the University of Strasbourg, which had then retreated to Clermont-Ferrand. In the rout from Alsace, the Alsatian students felt an overwhelming panic. They had no idea what they could do and what was going to happen to them. After a meeting of part of the faculty around the twentieth of June, I found myself in the foyer of the university, confronted with some fifty of these students. They interrogated me: "Tell us what we should do if the Germans arrive." I told them two things. First: "Under no conditions and no matter what the Germans do should you return to Alsace, because you will surely be put into the German army." And second: "The government that is forming around Marshal Pétain does not seem trustworthy to me. Therefore don't rely on whatever they might tell you."

Forty-eight hours later I was ordered to the police station, where the commissioner asked me if I had actually spoken these words. I unfortunately know which one of my students denounced me; the poor boy died on the Russian front wearing a German uniform. I replied that yes, I had made these remarks. I had to sign a statement. The commissioner was, by the way, very understanding, but at that time an investigation of me was begun, and they found out that my father was a foreigner. He had never become a citizen. As the son of a foreigner, I had to be fired. There you have it. So I was fired around the tenth of July. We left Clermont to return to Bordeaux where my family lived.

The second episode: three weeks later, in August, my father was ordered to appear before the German police. I remember that Bordeaux was occupied. I strongly urged him not to answer this summons and to "disappear." It would be insane to go, knowing how the Nazis were. My father replied, "No, I have nothing to worry about. I'm over seventy years old, and the international agreements prohibit the arrest of people over seventy." My father always trusted in laws. He thus went to the German military police station at the headquarters on rue Pessac, and he was immediately imprisoned without any further formality. I did what I could to find out what was happening to him and to free him. It was impossible. I saw him once through the bars, thanks to the kindness of a German guard.

Soon after my father was arrested, I learned from a friend who worked at police headquarters that my wife, who was born in Holland and had a British passport, was also going to be arrested. What choice did I have at that moment?

You see that it was not from a free political choice that I joined the Resistance. I had no alternative. In addition to all this, it is true that beginning in 1943 I really believed that the revolution was going to be possible.

And from 1940 to 1943?

At the beginning, as I mentioned before, the events had control over us. The way we left Clermont was rather amusing. We lived at the base of the plateau of Gergovie, in the country, naturally, because we have always lived in the country or the suburbs. And one fine day, we received a visit from the staff of General de Lattre, who was trying to regroup his division. The General explained to me: "I am installing my troops here. We are going to re-form the French army and block the German advance." That was very good, but it forced us to leave. I said to him: "I just lost my job. What do you think I should do?" "Well," he answered, "I'm going to give you a car, some gasoline, a driver, and a pass. Go wherever you wish." That's how we made it out. But we had to disappear from sight quickly.

Some friends had a small piece of property about forty kilometers from Bordeaux in a beautiful little hamlet called Martres, near Sauveterre-de-Guyenne. They rented it to us, and for four years we lived there and farmed it. It is sometimes said that French peasants are harsh. Well, these were admirable: they protected us. I had some exceptional friends there. Every time the police came and asked the mayor, "Do you have foreigners in the town?," he replied, "Yes, but don't worry about them. They are very good people, I will answer for them." Having always lived in a city and not knowing how to do anything but teach, I wasn't very clever at farming. They taught me everything.

And you actually farmed?

That's almost all I did. I grew potatoes and corn and raised sheep. My wife raised chickens and rabbits. The neighbors helped with everything. We lived from it, with our two children. But what we grew wasn't enough. We also needed "real money"; my wife's mother helped us out a bit. Later, I also worked for a specialist in the commercial court of law; he had me prepare reports. And then, in 1943, the school of law at Bordeaux very unofficially and without using my name gave me a small teaching assignment for the course in basic legal qualification. I put together all these incomes, and we managed to live. But the major part was farming.

And as soon as you could quit it, you did. Without regret?

My wife and I asked ourselves very seriously if we were going to give it up. My wife was for our staying. What made up my mind to come back was the political element. I believed it was going to be possible to carry out a large-scale political effort.

Was it in this little village in the Gironde region that you worked in the Resistance?

In reality I did very little—or for that matter, no—violent resistance. My first activity after disappearing was not at all to resist in order to chase out the German army or to cause destruction. No, it was the obligation to save some Jewish friends who were threatened with arrest, some people we knew. Later there were other Jews, false papers of all kinds, hideouts, and so on. Also, because our land was located almost exactly on the border between the occupied zone and the free zone, it made an excellent passage between the two. That is how it all developed, without any real political aim.

You said, however, that in 1943 you believed the revolution was near.

That's true. After the national council of the Resistance formulated its plan, we really believed for a year that the revolution was going to be possible. This was without a doubt one of my biggest errors in political judgment. I was really convinced that the 1943 slogan of the movement *Combat*—"From the Resistance to the revolution"—would become a reality. I thought that at the moment of the liberation all the political and economic structures would collapse, and we would have a clean slate just as we would for the reconstruction of the cities leveled by bombings. We were going to have a flexible social fabric. We were going to start almost from zero. All that was needed was readiness and daring, and the plan of the national resistance committee was daring. With new men and new institutions, what couldn't we do? Charbonneau never believed in it. He always refused to get involved in all that, telling me again and again that it was completely stupid, that it would never amount to anything at all. He had made a very lucid analysis of the situation. But I believed in it.

You believed, shall we say, that it was going to be possible to constitute a political system starting from scratch?

Precisely. And with new people. It was not only a question of constituting but also of organizing a new socioeconomic system outside of the traditional patterns. One of our propositions of that time was to start what we termed a "great workers' movement" at the moment of the liberation. The old socialist party and the old radicals would disappear to make room for a tremendous leftist movement. But I was told off by a leader of the socialist party; it was a dreadful experience. The socialist party was going to remain the socialist party. It was out of the question to touch it. But not only did the old parties and their local leaders take over again; it must also be said that the noncommunist resistance in France, the only free group, was caught at the time of the liberation between the communists and de Gaulle. They didn't have a chance. And the creation of the people's republican movement put an end to our hope of creating a great workers' movement. It was a great mistake.

After the liberation, you did nevertheless enter actively into politics.

At Bordeaux I took part in the liberation city council with Audeguil and Delaunay. It was very pleasant. We had a lot of work; we had to get everything back into working order.

How did you get onto this city council?

Since I was a member of a resistance group of the Gironde region and had good relations with everyone who had more or less played some role in the Resistance, they simply included me in the movement.

How long did you stay on it?

For about a year and a half.

Was it an important episode in your life?

Yes, in retrospect it was very important. Basically, this experience determined many of my later political and administrative analyses. I learned what little room for action a politician has and how heavy the administration is. And this was the case even during a troubled period, when from all appearances we were starting almost from scratch and the old structures were open to question. So that is where I learned, for example, how incredibly dependent we are on administrative departments. Since I had to re-examine and reorganize everything and I had thirty or forty matters arriving in my office, I went to city hall every day to work.

What particular area did you have charge of?

Each of us had five or six branches. And since it was obviously impossible for me, even working hard, to seriously study thirty issues during one day, I had to rely on the departmental heads. Now, by probing I found out several times that the reports were complete fabrications. They gave me files that were not based on serious technical studies, or they asked for my signature, just my signature, and that meant committing

myself to things that I didn't agree with at all. I finally
said to myself: if that's what it is like for a city coun-
cilman, what must it be like for a cabinet member who
receives not thirty files but three or four hundred? He
finds himself totally dependent upon the departments.

There is no power that doesn't delegate itself.

Undoubtedly, but then what you ought to do is to make
up the whole group of departments with your own
personnel, your supporters, and you must be entirely
sure that their assistants are able and intelligent, faithful and unambitious. Then at the point you are starting
to build the model of a technocracy, because these
departments will have everything at their disposition.
And what would your democratically elected successor
do? It's not as easy today as it was with the old American spoils system.[5]

But wasn't that the actual situation after the liberation?

Yes, to some degree, except that the jobs were dis-
tributed according to political nuances rather than
capabilities or personal trust. But I found myself confronted with some department heads whom I could not
trust. I was completely helpless.

So you gave up.

Yes, I gave up at the moment when an elected council
was to replace the old council; the latter had sort
of set itself up.

---

5. English in text.—TRANS.

Was that the elected council of Chaban-Delmas?

Yes, and I believe Chaban-Delmas would have liked for me to be a part of his council, but I was not at all enthusiastic about the idea of continuing on this political path. I had already moved away from it. I had no personal ambition, no desire to make politics my profession (besides, my wife and Bernard Charbonneau were strongly opposed to the idea), and during these months I had seen the powerlessness of politicians. As a result, I didn't see why I should continue—the goals I wanted to attain didn't seem to be attainable this way.

So this interlude in local politics was your only participation in the realm of government.

Exactly. The minister of the interior did actually offer to name me as a prefect, but I was not at all tempted. I really couldn't see myself holding a position of authority of this type.

All of your subsequent commitments were of a very different nature.

Very different. They were either in the realm of Christianity, shall we say, or in the social realm.

Did your disappointment from that political experience lead you to back away from a political commitment and especially from political commitment as a Christian, as I think your first book, published in 1947, shows?

Yes, in a sense. In fact, there were several of us who went into politics in 1944 with really new ideas, ready for a socioeconomic transformation. And we ran into such things as the territorial divisions of the traditional political parties: they remained exactly the same as before the war. The radical socialists and the major socialist party, especially, with their officials, thoroughly blocked everything. We arrived on the scene like choirboys with our sincerity, our certainties, and our revolutionary intransigence. And we found ourselves in company with some seasoned old foxes who knew how to conduct a political meeting and how to block it. The political networks were immediately reformed. Dating from this defeat and these manipulations, I developed a mistrust and even a hatred for political circles. I'm not just talking about the political ruling class but about the lower levels—the section and committee leaders on the local level. It is a terrible shame and a hopeless situation.

To sum it up, you lost your illusions. For this reason you broke with the political world. As far as anything in this life can be definitive, you have definitively broken with politics.

Try to understand me. I had seen the failure of the Popular Front in 1936; the failure of the personalist movement, which we intended to be revolutionary and which we tried to start on a modest scale; the failure of the Spanish revolution, which had great importance for Charbonneau and me; and the failure of the liberation. All of this formed an accumulation of ruined revolutionary possibilities. After this, I never believed anything could be changed by this route.

4.

The Revolutionary Gospel

MADELEINE GARRIGOU-LAGRANGE: *Did all of these failures and all of these experiences that touched you personally and also touched the whole of French society inspire or at least have an influence on your theological views?*

JACQUES ELLUL: I am glad you asked that question in that way and not, as is often done, in the opposite order. People tell me: "Because you are a Calvinist, you believe in innate evil, total depravity, and the fall of man, without any kind of positive characteristics to man." I don't believe that at all. First, I am not a Calvinist, and even though Calvin's writing influenced me some time ago, I have since moved away, quite far even, from his position.

Nevertheless, it is certain that the failure of almost all the efforts I was able to make in what I considered a revolutionary direction gave me a very strong feeling that this world is powerful, rigid, and cunning, and that radical political change is impossible in this world. Has this changed my theology? The funny thing is that when I think about it, I have progressed from a negative radicalism to a more open theology and, I think, a more humane one, during the last fifteen years. I don't think I'm getting soft, but I am less sectarian. In 1940 and again in 1945, I was theologically intransigent. I thought there was *one* theological truth. I don't believe that at all any more. I have developed in the direction of an openness. So the failure of my sociopolitical experiences hasn't hardened my theology.

I thought that the world is separated from God and therefore evil. I still believe it. But whereas I used to believe that God's judgment separated the lost, the condemned (to show God's justice), from others who were saved (to show God's love), I am now convinced that there is universal salvation, and I firmly believe that human history is leading to the new creation and the resurrection. Thus nothing is lost. If we fail on earth, we are not damned, it is only a great pity to continue to live badly and in hatred when one could perhaps live better and in friendship. I thus don't have a more pessimistic attitude than before, and likewise, this series of failures didn't send me running back to a religious consolation.

But didn't the failures at least guide your biblical study and cause, as we can see in your writing, this sort of dissociation between the life of faith and the political commitment as such? After all, if the revolutions you had hoped for had succeeded, you would perhaps have read the Bible from another perspective.

I don't know. But all the same I will remind you that long before these failures, one of my favorite theologians, next to Calvin, was Kierkegaard. They both led me to an understanding of the Bible that I wouldn't call pessimistic but at least radical and disruptive.

What do you mean by that?

That there is no possible continuity between man's actions on earth and God's establishment of his kingdom. Or in another way, that one can't obtain salvation —but this is already a part of orthodox Protestant thought—by an accumulation of works or by a successful spiritual life, and that man can't achieve good on his own. And I again have to clarify here. The good of which Scripture speaks is not the equivalent of moral goodness but a condition of conformity to God's will. And the good that any moral philosophy describes to us may not necessarily coincide with God's will as it is shown to us in the revelation. In other words, when we say that man can't do good on his own, it means that man can't do God's will without God.

I experienced all this at around the age of twenty-two or twenty-three, long before any political experiences. Of course, my approach to the Bible has been influenced by several factors in our society. For example, I developed a dialectical approach to the Bible not because I am a genius but because Hegel's and Marx's dialectics had been revived and because Barth himself was essentially a dialectical theologian. All of this was furnished me by the cultural milieu in which I developed. My cultural setting also gave me the critical method I applied to the Bible, that of not considering the text as inspired in each letter and comma.

Reciprocally, many of my major concerns were given to me by the environment I happened to be in. I would not have written a theology of the big city in the thirteenth century! I did it only because I found myself confronted with it. The milieu in which I lived and the experiences I had thus strongly influenced my approach to the Bible but not my fundamental interpretation of it.

On the other hand, your experiences led you to a decisive break with Marxism.

I would describe it more as a break with the ideology of Marxism. A break with the kind of Marxism that claims to be the aim of and the key to everything. On the other hand, I totally agree with a Marxism that offers a method of interpretation—one of the best interpretations, in fact, I believe the best—of the world of the nineteenth and twentieth centuries. I also agree with a Marxism that provides some opportunity for political action. All the while, I recognize the dangers of Marxism that were already present in Marx's writing.

Your present Marxism would thus be a Marxism of method and action but no longer one of faith.

I don't like the word faith applied to realities of this order. It is more a simple belief. Marxism as a sociological study of capitalism does not imply any belief. Belief comes into play, first, when Marxism takes on a messianic, revolutionary dimension (we want to believe in a happy-ever-after) and, second, when it is considered a science in every domain. In reality it is pure belief to call Marxism a science. This belief is always dangerous. I can no longer truly believe that Marxism represents the ultimate in science, the ultimate in truth. In these areas I would say that, on the contrary, when Marxism becomes dogmatic it is actually a lie.

Did you make this departure from Marxism after the war?

Oh, no. It had already been made earlier, in the sense that in the personalist movement, we already did not accept that Marx represented an ultimate truth. His is a penultimate truth. But I must say that, as some concrete, extremely concrete, experiences unfolded (the Spanish communists against the anarchists during the war; the activity of underground communists against the underground noncommunists in 1944), I broke away radically from communism. I can't understand why people waited until 1968[1] to open their eyes and

---

1. Summer of nationwide strikes and student riots.—TRANS.

see what communism is, any kind of communism (and not just Stalinism) in action and application. Imagine that a whole generation was deceived by the good fellowship of the Resistance. And even today, intellectuals accept criticism of communism in the areas of economics or institutions, but they are not the most important points. Communism is above all a radical corruption within humanity. That is what experience has taught me. In consequence, on the ideological level, Christian communists are the worst. Therefore, I am definitively opposed to communism.

Let's go back to the disillusionment that followed your short political career after the liberation. What was left for you to do?

After having had the impression that the political route led nowhere, I made a judgment that later proved itself as false as the preceding one. I said to myself, "After all, if Christians are awake, they should understand that society absolutely must be changed and that it is actually within their faith that a revolutionary movement should take seed, a movement that has nothing in common with the revolutionary bluff of the left-wing (or, of course, the right-wing, as the case may be)."

You said to yourself, "The Gospel is revolutionary."

It is basically revolutionary, more radical than other movements, and above all it contains the demand for a *permanent* revolution. I expressed this in fairly great detail in a chapter of one of my very first books (*The Presence of the Kingdom*, written in 1946): "Revolutionary

Christianity." In other words, we cannot be satisfied with changing just a constitution or a few structures. We must carry out a fundamental transformation of beliefs, of prejudices, and of presuppositions. We must do an iconoclastic work, destroying the false gods of our society. For I believe it is on this deep level that the revolution is decided, and not just in a modification of economic organization. But at the same time, we must have the courage and the lucidity for this questioning. All this seemed to me to be an inevitable consequence of the Gospel and the prophets, but not limited to an intellectual or ideological change; it necessarily implied a resulting sociopolitical revolution. This pointed me in the direction of activity within the Reformed Church. For example, with Jean Bosc we began to form after the war what we called "Protestant professional associations." They were not intended to defend professional interests but to present people who practiced a profession with an ethical imperative that the Bible can provide for any job or profession. We thought that if we managed to revolutionize professional practices, change would begin there and would probably spread in a decisive manner to entire segments of society. Because professions and work have such importance in society, in changing them we could not help but turn society upside down.

Did you have a precise plan or did you think that the plan would sort of emerge by itself?

To our thinking, the plan should not be pre-arranged but be born of a renewed professional practice. We were already using a method that was later further developed. It employed a very concrete study of the professional situation and placed in opposition to this in a dialectical fashion the biblical or theological imperative.

A moral imperative?

Yes, an ethic, if you will, but not an ethic of commandment expressed in a "Thou shalt." It is, rather, a spiritual ethic: here is the imperative that is revealed to us; how do we change the situation in order to obey this imperative? Now, despite the ideas people have of it, this imperative is never a "Thou shalt/thou shalt not" but an imperative of liberty beginning with liberation by Christ.

Once again, as before the war, you went back to the formula of small groups.

We had a large number of these groups and they worked very intensely.

Only in the Protestant world?

Yes. But that didn't make matters any easier. Some of them were totally rebellious. We started a group of insurance agents and a group of bankers. Well, they did not even meet a second time. From the first meeting, I was faced with a brick wall. We began with such a fundamental criticism of the very concept of insurance, and insurance is such an integral part of a capitalist society, that the Gospel challenge proved to be unacceptable. They rejected it completely. The groups that

worked the best, obviously, were groups of social workers, doctors, nurses, and teachers. We had an appreci-
able influence in the teaching population. The groups
functioned for four or five years, and then we realized
that we were not yet approaching a fundamental transformation of society.

*You came to the conclusion that there are pure occupations
and impure ones.*

Absolutely not. That would be a return to the morality
of "Thou shalt/thou shalt not" that is anti-Christian.
No occupation is impure or prohibited. But since certain practices become impossible for the person who
gives his entire life to God, and since those practices
are sometimes inevitable in certain occupations, there
is no free choice of whether one is to do them or not,
and the profession *almost* becomes an impossible choice.
But this remains a personal decision, absolutely not
along the lines of a list of good occupations and bad
ones. I knew a bar owner who was a remarkable Christian and who made his bar a real place of witness!

But can a Christian be a banker?

I can only give my personal opinion. As far as I am
concerned, no, I could never be a banker, and even less
a politician. Considering that I didn't have a very
strong desire to become a member of the house of
representatives or a cabinet member, I know easily
what obstacle would have prevented me, in any case,
from coveting such a job: I would have had to make
decisions strictly incompatible with my world view or

with my faith in Jesus Christ. And, if I had not made
these decisions, I would have been a lousy politician.

*Did you think in those days that these groups of Christians
could have a sort of underground influence that could possibly transform the world and thus eliminate from your orientation any need for a global political plan? Or did you leave
this planning for others to do?*

At that time, I didn't yet leave it to others. I thought
that global political plans were ineffective and that
only by working inside society, in this professional
domain that is so decisive, could we succeed in changing the conditions we live in. I was in fact more interested in living conditions than in institutional structures. Of course, in all of this, it was never a question of
giving up on transforming society, but rather the belief
that trying to achieve it by political means is a dead
end; that one can really accomplish nothing by that
route; and that we must act from other angles, in the
areas left untouched by politicians, through means
outside of political parties, and with more basic objectives that catch the politicians off balance.

For you, this represented a significant change in goal.

Yes, it was a great change—that's certain—and a huge
undertaking.

A change motivated by some bitterness—

Oh, no! This is something that often surprises those
who interview me. I will readily admit that I have failed

everywhere, but I don't nurse any bitterness over it. I don't believe any of my actions have ever been motivated by bitterness or resentment. A phrase of Paul's from the First Epistle to the Corinthians had an enormous influence on me: "Paul planted, Apollos watered, but God gave the growth." I have had this outlook since 1944. Before, I was less detached from the results of my actions. But since, I have acquired the certainty that I must do all that is to be done, as the preacher of Ecclesiastes said, "Whatever your hand finds to do, with all your strength, do it." On the other hand, whether or not it succeeds is no longer my affair; God will make things grow or he will not make them grow. If they should not grow, well, that is too bad, that's all I can say before trying something else. All my life, I've tried something else.

In reading your books, one has the impression that you are warning people, saying, "Look out, this paticular area is a mine field."

Yes, I always write about my experience and about it alone, and I try to draw the lesson, saying, "Here there's nothing to be done." For example, if I sometimes react violently on the subject of the Ecumenical Council, it is because of the experience I had there that taught me that at the present time we can hope for very little real spiritual progress from the council and also that its sociopolitical studies and messages are pretty worthless.

You are pointing out the wastelands you have crossed.

I believe so firmly in initiative and in the capacity of
invention that I would not want someone to repeat the
mistakes I made. That is what I mean when I tell young
men of twenty to twenty-five years old, "Don't do that.
From my experience it leads nowhere; find something
new." Since my experience did not obtain results, it
was not what should have been done. Let's not waste
our time; we'll try to find something else. Unfortunately, I have become very skeptical at this point. I
have learned that the experience of elders almost never
helps. The most striking example is that of communism:
the experience of the Moscow trials turned some away.
Then there was the German-Soviet pact, as well as the
massacre of anarchists in Spain: this turned away the
best minds from the French Communist party, but their
experience, their warnings, had no effect. Nor did the
tragedy of East Berlin in 1953, nor the invasion of
Prague, nor the repression in 1956 and then in 1968,
and even now, there are always the naive who join the
party without listening to those who have lived in this
world and have ended up discouraged. But we must
always begin again.

*And you have done just that, since 1944, in several
battlefields.*

Exactly.

*You have fought a battle on two fronts in your writing and in
your action: the front of intellectual battle and the front of
concrete battle.*

You could put it that way.

5.

Writing for Battle

MADELEINE GARRIGOU-LAGRANGE: *Time and time again you have seen action on all sorts of fronts: some of them in the religious sphere, others in the secular sphere. I will name a few: the church and the university, juvenile delinquents, the development of the Aquitaine region. Your written work also very much resembles a battle. I am wondering how all of this ties together. What induced you, at around the age of thirty, to embark on such a program?*

JACQUES ELLUL: First of all, as many people have told me, I am by nature a man of action. I always think in terms of interventions, and if something does not lead to action, it doesn't interest me. In other respects, gifted as I was with a good working mind, I became an intellectual.

The tie between these two elements led me to the lifestyle I have adopted. And here again, my friend Charbonneau had a decisive influence. He embodied both a reproach of my failure as a Christian to follow the urgent commandment, "You must do something," and a critical glance that said, "What you are doing means nothing." I tried to rescue the Christian faith from his criticism through my commitments.

But you and he did not share the same vision.

No, of course not, insofar as we disagreed from the beginning, sometimes very strongly, in the area of faith. If this certainty had not been given me, I would never have been able to take action in any domain.

What certainty?

That of the biblical revelation. Without it, I would have foundered in despair from seeing the uselessness of my efforts and the failure of all the revolutions. Failure has always had great importance in my life. I witnessed the failure of 1936,[1] of the Spanish revolution, of the Resistance, of 1968, and of my personal undertakings. But because I firmly believe that God is the ultimate, that he is grace, that he continually renews everything, and that he has promised to recapitulate everything

---

1. A short-lived coalition of socialists and communists under Léon Blum was elected to power.—TRANS.

through a positive fulfillment of history at the end of time, I have never despaired. Every time I have received the impetus necessary to begin again. That's all.

Would you describe your intellectual and literary project as you conceived of it at that time?

Well, it took place during the occupation. I asked myself what mode of action would be possible after the war and in what areas action was needed. This implied a sociological analysis of the situation. In another respect, I felt that one could not seriously be a Christian intellectual without a good theological education. I had these two interests that did not coincide: to do a sociological study of society with the aim of eventual action, and to deepen my faith as a Christian intellectual through theological study.

Did these two areas really have nothing in common? Is theology so unconcerned with what happens to man in society?

The purpose of theology for me was, first, to arrive at as truthful as possible a knowledge and understanding of the biblical text. It thus consists of exegetical research, mastering Hebrew, learning the various interpretations, reading the church fathers.

Isn't that very intellectual and abstract?

Yes, but if one does not have this knowledge of Scripture, one cannot formulate theology and be a

Christian intellectual. I tried to answer as well as I could this call that challenged me fairly early as a Christian: "You will love the Lord your God with all your heart, and with all your soul, and with all your strength, and *with all your mind.*" What does that mean, to love with your mind? What use of the mind, or of knowledge, what direction should one take, what liberation or what obedience? These were my questions.

You thus gave yourself an enormous program of study.

Little by little I became convinced that it was enormous and, moreover, that it could not be two separate areas of research, that some kind of relationship between them should be possible. What relationship? I thought there could be a kind of dialectical relation. Not that for a problem stated in sociological terms there exists a Christian response, but that there exists a dialectical counterpoint. When one has grasped the two elements, one should be able to progress both in knowledge and in action.

Therefore I tried in 1943 to formulate a plan for what would be a study of contemporary society, with the theological counterpoint in parallel. As I was not in the least a theoretician, it seemed indispensable to me to develop an ethic and to find elements in the biblical text itself that shed light on present situations.

Beginning with the basic theme of Technique—here again, Bernard Charbonneau had, as early as 1935, grasped the key role of Technique and started me in that direction—it was necessary to find the relationship between politics and Technique, between psychological factors and Technique; to find the future of man in an increasingly technicalized society; and so on. This was one of the great orientations of my work, the other being the understanding furnished by the Bible and the means by which mankind can manage to live humanely in the modern context.

Once again, it was not a question of giving Christian responses or solutions (which would be absurd). How can we propose solutions derived from our faith to people who live outside the faith? But more important, the Bible is not a recipe book or an answer book, but the opposite: it is the book of questions God asks us. So it was necessary to find which questions are pertinent for our society today. Neither experience nor sociology could teach me this: to find the questions and also the reasons to live *in spite of everything.*

Thirty-five years later, these are still the orientations of your work, aren't they?

I am glad that people have begun to realize that, because I have never said it, I've never given an explanatory guide to my writing. I waited for readers to take the initiative and find their own explanations.

So you had a project, one that was coherent, in your opinion. And now time has passed. You are still progressing in these two directions with your dialectical method. With the changes in the world and all that has happened in these thirty-five years, have your studies brought some surprises in taking you somewhere other than where you had planned?

Not very many. When it comes right down to it, the most tragic thing in these developments is this: for forty years I have always written or spoken to predict what could happen, in order to warn others of what was likely to happen. I had hoped that people would take it seriously enough to really take charge of their history rather than be carried away by events, by the course of nature. But almost every time and in almost every domain, events have confirmed what I had predicted. Now, I can't be happy about it, or proud of myself, because I wrote so that things *wouldn't* turn out that way. It happened as I said, but not as I wished! I have always found myself in a situation you may find strange: I worked with the goal that subsequent events would prove me wrong. Being right was only evidence to me that I had failed. I hadn't known what to do to change the course of our society. I started over. But I didn't have very many surprises—no, that's not true. I did have some. The agreeable surprise of 1968. The disagreeable surprise of seeing that a great number of people are concerned today about the problems of the technicalized society but that my studies of twenty-five or thirty years ago are ignored. People are inspired by them, quote them, but forget to give credit.

I have changed more from a theological standpoint than from a sociological one. I have not transformed, so much as clarified and furthered, my intuitive knowledge of society.

Nothing that has happened in the past thirty-five years has caused me to change anything basic in my original thinking. My explanatory keys and work methodology have remained the same, and so-called new developments in the world have only confirmed what I have written.

But didn't these events and what they taught you cause you to develop in the area of theology?

I would say that two developments have come about. First, a deeper knowledge of the Bible, one that is more and more free from philosophical or theological presuppositions. And then—is it sentimentality that comes with age?—I have an increasingly keen sensitivity to human ordeals. Before, when I tried to show how this society was restrictive, how it was the cause of our difficulties, I thought of human beings in the abstract. My work with juvenile delinquents put me in contact with such great distress, distress more psychological and spiritual than physical, that my theology was very strongly influenced.

For example, I think the theology of universal salvation that I came to believe in—thus scandalizing my Calvinist friends—is fundamentally biblical. But it also expresses the impossibility of God rejecting those who live in such distress without ever having any opportunity to meet him. This represents a considerable change in my theological perspective, as was my certainty that an encounter with Jesus Christ is to be found not only through a clear explanation of the faith but also through the context of real life. It is absolutely impossible for me to believe any longer in double predestination. And though I still believe that knowledge and recognition of Jesus Christ are essential, I no longer think they are necessary for salvation but rather for hope, for a break with the past, for openness, for a newness in living; no matter what the past has been, God's call to mankind marks a new beginning.

Insofar as I have come to this certainty of a universal salvation, an explicit confession of faith in Jesus Christ is not the condition for salvation. Salvation is always, for everyone, by grace. In other words, to use the theological terms, the soteriological dimension is diminished with respect to the dimension of the kingdom, this kingdom where all humanity will enter, without exception. It has already begun here.

If this be the case, is it worth the trouble to proclaim Jesus Christ and to talk of him? I answer yes without hesitation, for when I encounter individuals in total despair, crushed by misfortune, by the lack of a future, by injustice or loneliness, I must transmit to them the reason I myself have found to hope and to live. In other words, the message is no longer, "Be converted or I will kill you," but rather, "You want to kill yourself; be converted to escape from killing yourself."

At one time in your life you believed in a hell.

It was consistent with certain biblical texts that speak of the separation between the good and the bad. But they must be correctly understood.

You have ceased to believe in the God of Calvin, the God of predestination.

Based on God's foreknowledge, Calvin presented a two-sided God: a side of love and a side of justice. And justice should be expressed in the damnation of those who are created for damnation.

God didn't throw a weight onto the scale to make it lean toward the good side?

That is his loving side. He saves by grace, otherwise we would all be damned. In other words, the whole world is damned, and God saves some by grace, thus demonstrating the nature of love and grace. For the others, he allows his justice to operate. I had not yet fully understood what Péguy meant when he said: "If there were only justice, who could then be saved; but there is mercy and because there is mercy, who then can claim that he is not saved?" *(Mystère des saints innocents)*[2] and "how God does nothing except out of mercy."[3]

When you were converted, was it these writings on the faith that convinced you?

No, it was from reading the Bible.

With Calvin's narrow interpretation.

It was from reading the Bible. Calvin seemed to me to give the most clear account of what I had read in the Bible. But I have to admit that there was also an element of rebellion, of hatred of certain political actions that naturally made me divide the world in two. I

---

2. Epic poem about Joan of Arc by Catholic, socialist, and nationalist Charles Péguy (1912).—TRANS.

3. Péguy (1914): litany to Eve, exhorting her to pray for "us, carnal beings like you."—TRANS.

couldn't accept salvation for Nazis, and later, for communists. They seemed to me totally outside of God's love. Therefore Calvin was right. But very quickly Jean Bosc introduced me to Barth, who has a completely different outlook. I recall the shock I had in 1936—or perhaps it was 1935—in reading *The Word of God and the Word of Man.* It happened at about the same time that I discovered *Esprit.* And it was an incredible liberation.

How did Barth shake up your convictions?

First, I discovered through him a flexible comprehension of Scripture. Barth was infinitely less systematic than Calvin, and he was completely existential at a time when this concept did not exist. He put biblical thought in direct contact with actual experience; it wasn't armchair theology.

And then Barth did something I found phenomenal. Within Protestantism at that time there was a strong trend labeled liberal; it was somewhat similar to the old Catholic modernism. It had a tendency to eliminate from Christianity and theology anything that was not rationally and scientifically acceptable. As for me, I was not at all liberal, in the sense that I valued above all else the biblical text, in which everything, including the irrational and the nonscientific, seemed important to me. Still, the criticism of liberals seemed serious to me (especially the historical criticism). Barth went beyond the orthodox-liberal controversy, and he did it by means of a dialectic, integrating into his theology everything the liberals had discovered and formulated.

In particular he reintegrated the myth as a means of comprehending the biblical text. Now, at this time the myth was considered to be equivalent to legend or even fabrication. Myths were stories that should be ignored. . . .This was a significant discovery for me. Finally, it became possible to proceed in the direction of a scientific, historical, exegetical, and critical research, all the while maintaining the completeness of the biblical text. Even better, this research allowed me to be more seriously faithful to Scripture and did not contradict the inspiration of the Holy Spirit. This is the first feature that inspired me in Barth's writings.

Another element was very important: the way in which Barth puts mankind back into theology. As a result of one of these familiar contradictions, the theology of grace—not with Calvin but with Calvinists—had succeeded in eliminating the human element, because a theology of grace that totally denies works leads to total pessimism. If we are totally sinners and our works will never be worth anything, we can only receive salvation by grace. Thus it is useless to do anything. It is very interesting to note that in practice, things didn't happen this way. The Calvinist Protestants were extremely active in all domains, in commerce as well as politics or the military, and usually they were very successful. There are several possible explanations. According to some, the Calvinists considered, on the basis of several verses, that success in worldly affairs was a benediction from God. Now, this was important, for belief in predestination is absolutely no guarantee that one is among those predestined to be saved. There is no way of being certain, since works are of no use. But if success in business is the sign of benediction, from that point on . . .

According to Bernard Charbonneau, this attitude came from the fact that the Calvinist God is so transcendent, the separation between this God and man is so great that, after all, one can do as one pleases on this earth, at least to some degree. I couldn't believe that. It seemed to me that bringing about the revolution and changing society were essential, and at the same time I was well aware that the theology of grace was true. Barth went beyond that. He maintained a theology of grace in showing that the God who is gracious is at the same time the God who liberates us, and we are liberated not to make ourselves happy but to live effectively, to be in the world, to go everywhere bearing liberty.

To show that liberty is essential and that God is the liberator is an important goal in Barth's thinking. Beginning with his thinking, one could say that everything is turned around. God's commandments are no longer imperatives, but promises. We should no longer read in the Ten Commandments, "You must do this," but rather, "You will have the possibility of living like this." It is the future tense of grace: from the moment your life is turned around by grace, you will no longer be able to kill, to steal, to lie. A path is opened up before you. God is he who continually frees us from all that hinders. He is only warning us when he says, "If you go beyond, you will not find me (with my terrifying side and my damnation), but you will find death. If you begin to kill, you will be killed." Thus it is not a harsh restriction that keeps us from going beyond the limits, but a possibility of life.

In other words, God gives us free rein.

Much more: he opens before us the doors to new possibilities while we constantly close them. This was, besides, one of the great transformations effected by Barth's theology in that he showed how human freedom works within God's freedom. God is sovereignly free; he gives grace to whom he gives grace, he reveals himself to whom he reveals himself, and he intervenes as he wishes. And, within this immense freedom, he acts as liberator, saying to mankind, in the words of Paul, "All things are lawful, but not all things are helpful. You can do all things, but not all things edify." In other words, we are embarked upon a path of invention and not of repetition. It is up to us to make what we can of it.

Evil is repetition?

Biblically, theologically, and spiritually, repetition *is* an evil because it is the refusal to begin, that is to say, to—be converted. Of course, I am using the word *repetition* here in a very different sense from the repetition of Kierkegaard.

Isn't Cain the precise opposite of a repetitious man? He is the one who breaks out of the endless repetition of the pastoral world to create the city. And he does all this because God condemned him.

But God never condemned Cain: that is a widely held

misconception. It is true that he makes a new beginning. Opposite the beginning established by God (which he continually renews), Cain establishes *his* beginning (the Hebrew words of the text say this expressly). It is the beginning of man without God (but man will make gods for himself), and even man against God, because Cain refuses everything: the protection God promises him and the future God lays out for him. Cain wants to make *his* own world (the city) from which he will exclude God. But the biblical myth tells us immediately that this particular beginning was not the beginning of liberty, it was the beginning of necessity, the beginning of an inescapable chain of events, of fate. But God never gives up, and at the same time he never constrains or imposes himself. Thus at the end of history he reworks even our most proud and rebellious inventions. That is why, by the way, I have not lost hope in the face of Technique. It would be a tragedy if we ended up becoming totally mechanized robots. I have always fought to keep that from happening.

But as long as we are not completely adapted to Technique, ill at ease with it, we will invent new things and God will listen to what we invent. When God does not speak, he is always listening. And everything that we in our anguish and misery hope for, God will fulfill.

At the end of time, we will obtain the complete fulfillment of all we have hoped for. That is why I am, if I can express it in this way, utterly optimistic. Nothing of our past history, nor of our present history, nor of our future history, is or will be lost: no human cry, no human hope, no human despair. God collects everything. And with what he is collecting he will make and

give us the world to come, the heavenly Jerusalem. We
will build it with our efforts as God answers them.

Going back to your personal life, you have tried to invent—

I have undertaken my own invention and my own
path. In any case, it seemed impossible to me to live
without a meaning to life. I definitely had to find one.
Even if there is no intrinsic meaning.

And you found it in action?

Because I have a realistic and active nature, meaning
lay in action. But it is obvious that, for me, action itself
does not embody meaning. Action more or less gives
witness to meaning, expresses it to me or to others. But
the most basic meaning is beyond all action. As Ricoeur
said: "There is a surplus of meaning."[4] And I live on this
surplus.

---

4. Paul Ricoeur, French Christian and existentialist philosopher of
the twentieth century. —TRANS.

6.

The Church
and the Spirit

MADELEINE GARRIGOU-LAGRANGE: *To act, to accomplish, and to fight are one and the same to you. You have for a long time waged a real battle within your church.*

JACQUES ELLUL: I was persevering, I can say that much. I remained for twenty-one years on the national council of the Reformed Church of France, which is approximately the equivalent of the council of bishops of the Catholic Church. Jean Bosc and I had observed that the professional associations had got bogged down. Since we thought everything should be based on people's initiatives, we didn't give them advice: "Here's what you must do." That was not our aim; they needed to find their own style of working, to invent. After five years, they continued to be bottle-fed with what Jean Bosc gave them and didn't show themselves capable of maturing, so we gave up. That's when I thought of joining the national council.

Once again with the purpose of changing the course of events.

To try. And it was another great undertaking, trying in a way to transform the Reformed Church into an active movement within society. This was my goal, but to begin with, the church had to be transformed.

Did you have a clear idea of what this church could become?

Certainly. That is an important question, for even though I always refused either to develop a plan for society or to work politically for a certain model of society, thinking that it should germinate within society itself, we did, on the contrary, see rather clearly what the church should be.

"We?"

Jean Bosc and I. We shared the same point of view in working on two different levels, Jean on that of theological change and I on an attempt at institutional change, both of us having the goal of mobilizing this church.

Basically, I was always searching for motivations that could lead people to make revolutionary decisions.

It was never with the intent of starting a mass movement or of getting people to join for superficial or
emotional reasons. We felt that the decision to act
comes through an awakening as completely as possible
to a situation. I thought at that time that the Protestant
church could develop this awakening and create in all
Protestants who consider themselves serious Christians
enough motivation for them to intervene in society and
transform its cultural and mythical structures. Moreover, I was attached to the church, not passionately but
relatively, and several of us in 1950 sensed the approaching crisis.

These two elements—the desire to make Christians
wake up and to mobilize them, and the necessity to
ward off the crisis—resulted in the creation, around
1955, of a special committee of the Reformed Church:
the committee on strategy.

A name that says a lot.

A somewhat pretentious name that, by the way, provoked some violent reactions from Protestants who
only think of things in terms of the individual and
reject the idea that the church can have a strategy.

Since it was first necessary to ascertain the actual
state of our forces, we undertook a statistical inventory
that was as thorough as possible. And we found to our
amazement that the figure of one million Protestants in
France—the classical, usual, recent, average figure—
was nothing but a legend. We found three hundred
thousand serious members.[1] For those who learned of it,
it was a pretty heavy psychological blow.

---

1. Note in 1980: It is evident that we are a long way from the two

The Protestants were nothing more than a small remnant.

Exactly. The second action of the committee on strategy consisted of studying how to make God's people aware of the global problems of society. Roughly, the question was as follows: What is threatening mankind? Not what threatens Christians or the Christian faith in particular, but human beings in society.

Furthermore, the church's structures were heavy and rigid. We wanted to make them flexible and allow people to become mobilizable in the etymological sense of the word, that is, mobile and able to commit themselves.

We thus undertook the reform of the church's structures, only proposing truly feasible changes. And we elaborated seven great outlines covering the reorganization of the local parish, the relations between the parish and what we call the council of elders, the question of informing the church, that of authority in the church. There was also a plan for progressive application of these measures.

We were in reality very episcopalian, for we realized that although the Protestant system of councils is reliable (perhaps not very democratic), it is very sluggish. Imagine—the simplest question circulates among the various councils for about eighteen months before obtaining a response. We needed something more flexible and more active. It took us years to develop this plan,

---

million people identifying themselves as Protestants or interested in Protestantism given in a recent poll regarding Protestants. But I am still convinced that in 1980, as in 1960, there are about three hundred thousand Protestants really tied to the church.

which failed totally because the rank-and-file Christians in the church did not understand it.

Were they well informed?

We had done as serious and complete a work of informing as possible. We used all available means: the press, lectures, opinion polls. And we met with three types of reactions. First, the familiar refrain, "You are practicing politics in the church," whereas the plan aimed at intervention in the framework of society. Others felt that this had nothing to do with the faith, and most of them displayed a complete indifference, having no idea of the real problems of our time (outside of political questions) and possessing only a weak spiritual character.

Did they perhaps feel your activity was an attempt to enlist them in a political activity?

Yes, they could have felt that way. But we had the opposite intentions. We wanted each Christian layman to become aware of his or her responsibility as a Christian in this society. But we ran into a big problem: Protestantism is founded on individual faith and on individual interpretation of Scripture, and we were asserting the necessity of moving from a faith that should be individual to a joint action, or in theological terms, from preaching only salvation to preaching the kingdom. This, Protestants did not understand.

In following Barth, Cullmann, and Visscher we were led to this transposition: that Jesus Christ is not only Savior, he is also Lord. And we have to find out how

this lordship is expressed today in the world, taking
into account that the kingdom of God is not only a
future reality but also a dimension already present and
active in this world. This aspect is often ignored by
traditional Reformed theology and was a cause of the
negative or indifferent reaction of Protestantism as a
whole.

At the top level as well as at the bottom?

No. This principle interested the leaders very much,
and many pastors committed themselves in this direction. But this had an undesired institutional result. I
mentioned that we were episcopalian. The presidents
of regional councils experienced an increase in their
powers, but in a direction I would call (to be a bit nasty)
legalistic and bureaucratic. They had a tendency to
become the same thing the bishops were criticized for
being fifty years ago: managers rather than mainsprings
behind a mobilization of the church for action within
society.

*If I understand correctly, you had wanted to mobilize the
base and it was the top that mobilized. Wasn't this a repetition for you, this time in an ecclesiastical setting, of what
you had experienced in the political domain after the
liberation—a takeover by bureaucrats?*

Yes, essentially; that's pretty exact. It became evident
at the moment when elections replaced the president
of the national council and changed a large part of the
council. The new members knew nothing of what we

had been preparing for several years (which was finished and ready to be set in motion); without studying
the question, with a flick of the wrist they brushed it all
aside.

It represented the total failure of our conception of a
church strategy, in which we put a heavy emphasis on
Christianity's specificity. We were convinced—and this
conviction has only continued to grow with me—that
a society is composed of sympathies and various trends
and that this multiplicity is necessary to it; that society
is all the more alive because contradictions result between all of these trends; and that Christians offer to
society something that no one else is capable of giving.
There is a basic conflict in Protestantism: should Christians join existing movements, those that are most just;
should they, for example, side with the poor man; or
does Christianity have something really specific and
unique that should not be mixed up with anything else?
Does God want to carry out a different action in history
through Christians, who consequently don't need to
adopt ready-made plans and doctrines? I am totally in
favor of the second perspective, but of course I have
already said so. It is not a matter of founding a party or a
Christian labor union or of uniting Christians around a
social doctrine of the church. Nor is it that Christians
should join any particular political party. It is that they
should carry on a specific activity on a particular level
where they can apply the question I mentioned a while
ago: what is threatening mankind today?

*According to you, on this level Christians have special
insight.*

I wouldn't say that they have special insight. I no longer think that one can derive from the Bible a political or social doctrine that is more true than others. But Christians will have a special courage, a spirit of inventiveness, a lucidity, a radicality, an ability to change, a desire for justice and liberty, all of which come from the Gospel and which no one else can have, if—they accept the consequences of their faith, if they accept transformation within. I believe that Christians can be, among other things, more realistic and less ideological than others, contrary to what is commonly believed. And I explain this in the following manner: it is because we have the certainty of the kingdom of God. In other words, no reality, no matter how terrible or how hard it may be, can make us lose hope. Knowing that God has always kept his promises, that Jesus is already resurrected, that his victory over death is already won, that the kingdom of God is promised and will be accomplished, we must see reality without any kind of illusion. Marxism is purely illusory. Faith in Christ doesn't have to be.

This is not optimism. It is the certainty of faith: faith that, through the crucifixion of Jesus Christ, the powers of this world have been conquered; that through the resurrection of Jesus Christ, death is conquered; that all God's promises are inevitably fulfilled; and that we are promised the kingdom. I can thus say: everything is done. Everything except history. History is no small thing, and we must make it.

Do you believe that after God was incarnated, his presence in the world has remained the same as in the Old Testament?

I am absolutely sure that there is a continuity. But whether it is a matter of his presence or of his turning away, of his word or of his silence, the only difference is that in Jesus Christ we have received the irrevocable certainty that, no matter what happens, God loves all of us more than we can ever know. However, when Jesus tells us, "I am with you always, to the end of the world," he does not at all mean that he guarantees his presence in the midst of us like a piece of furniture. At the beginning of the Book of Revelation, the Lord, who holds in his hand seven stars that are the seven churches, announces to one of them, "If you continue, I will leave you."

We have to admit that the regions of the world that used to be very Christian—North Africa, Turkey, and all of Asia Minor—have ceased to be Christian. It is very possible that Christianity will change location again, that Europe will cease to be Christian, while Indonesia will become Christian. Nevertheless, I live in Europe and in France, so I am responsible for this particular church and for God's word that must be proclaimed to the men of my country. No matter what God's decision may be, I ought to do everything exactly as if it will all continue.

As a historian, do you feel, then, that God has intervened in twenty centuries of Christianity as we see him intervene in the Bible?

Without a trace of doubt. For example, I cannot conceive that Saint Francis could have caused, as he did, the movement that started with him. He was truly inspired by God, who, through him, worked in the church. And many more besides Saint Francis. I would include Luther, too.

God works through all kinds of prophets.

Always through people. For me, God is never the deus ex machina who resolves all problems. He sends us and we do what we can. If we fail, it's a failure. And God starts over.

And now you seem to believe that God is silent, that he sends no more people.

It is very possible. And it is tragic. It is possible that God is allowing us to follow our own path of madness, but it is also possible that he is awakening people and no one is listening to them or joining with them. In the domain of theology, it seemed likely that Barth was this awaited prophet. But now, several years after his death, we see the eclipse of Barthian thought. In the same vein, the extraordinary opening made by Vatican II has strangely closed back up or been turned aside.

The same phenomenon occurred after Saint Francis of Assisi.

That is the very reason that I say that history is never decided, either positively or negatively. We have to make this history, that of the church as well as that of the world.

You nevertheless have the conviction that we are living in a special age, that God has turned away from the world today. Why?

First, there is my experience with the Reformed Church, which should be a charismatic church, a church traditionally flexible. And we find that every effort to restore inspiration to the church and above all to begin an action in society falls flat, for institutional reasons. I will make a rather severe comparison here. When we see Jesus Christ or the Holy Spirit act, a tremendous number of things come out of very little: look at the feeding of the five thousand. In the church we observe just the opposite: we put excellent men into action and we mount gigantic efforts that produce almost nothing. So I say to myself, "This means that the Holy Spirit is not working."

I have often watched what took place at the national council. I worked with some remarkable people. But day after day passed in which nothing was accomplished. That is not at all the equivalent of Pentecost.

Aren't you of the opinion that the Holy Spirit rarely manifests himself in the church hierarchy and that he has preferred to go off the beaten path, as with Saint Francis of Assisi?

Of course. And all my life I have looked for these alternate paths. But to come back to the reason I think we live in a special period, I would like to bring up another experience I had: the impossibility of achieving a real transformation of the structures of this world, both in the political as well as the economic domains. These structures are extremely restrictive, it is true, but if we don't master them, who can, and how? I see only a process of repetition and reinforcement of the worst tendencies. Communism under a facade of justice is worse than everything that preceded it. And 1968 made matters worse. Everything is continually being repeated, recycled.

Our emphasis in the national council was thus on the specific contribution Christians could offer in all these difficulties: realism, as I said, and then hope that all determinism or appearance of determinism is already conquered. In other words, mankind cannot allow itself to be crushed by economic, political, or any other kind of determinism; on the contrary, we have a decisive reason to commit ourselves all the way. Then, of course, we must do it with lucidity.

Long before Moltmann published his theology of hope, we thought that the Christian's calling was to bring hope to humanity. This obviously did not exclude participation in a labor union or a party, as long as the Christian had a different role to play there.

Now that your project for the Reformed Church has failed, what do you expect from this church?

It would be unkind of me to say I don't expect much from it as a church. I am still a member, but I don't think the church can produce an important innovation on any level. On the other hand, I still believe very firmly in the preaching of the Gospel in and by this church, on two conditions: that the church be pluralistic, that is, not having within it theological trends that are likely to exclude all others, but rather having dialogues between differing individuals; second, that the church open itself to relations with the other great church, the Catholic Church, and with the Jews. With these conditions, the Reformed Church has its own role and its specificity. On the other hand, I no longer believe in its force of impact on society nor in the awakening it could stimulate.

For you personally, it has ceased to be a field of battle and of study.

It is a church where I have friends, where I like to be, to preach, to hear preaching and take communion. I will stay there. But I am more a member of a local church, a parish, than a member of the national Reformed Church.

Why did you describe yourself as on the sidelines of it?

Basically, between 1960 and 1970 I took positions that put me on the sidelines. The conflict centered on two points. First, I was hostile to the politicization of the church, the primacy of politics; I was violently against a well-known slogan: "Seek first the political kingdom, and all these things will be added unto you." Concretely, it was with the war in Algeria, when I disagreed with the positions taken by the church leaders, that I was set apart.

Following that came the period when the popular opinion held that Christianity should be expressed above all in service—a total but single-minded commitment. As for me, I maintained that service means nothing if there is not an explicit proclamation of the message of Jesus Christ as Lord and Savior. The proclamation of the Word can only be made through the word. Witnesses are those who speak and put their words to work. Well, these two orientations were completely rejected by Protestant intellectuals and then by the leaders of the church. From that point on—

7.

The Christian Is
Always One Step Ahead

MADELEINE GARRIGOU-LAGRANGE: *You have said that you preached and that you like to preach. Yet you are not a pastor, are you?*

JACQUES ELLUL: No, I am not officially a pastor, but I sometimes fulfill the role temporarily in our small parish of Pessac. In coming here to settle down, my wife and I were in a way the "Christianizers" of this parish.

Did the parish exist before your arrival?

There were a few Protestant families, but no church.

To use the words of those days, we brought up this church. Until then, Pessac was attached to the parish of Talence, a large parish. About ten people were meeting here at Pessac each month. When we arrived, the pastor at Talence said to us, "It's wonderful. I've been waiting for years for someone able to take responsibility in Pessac, because I can't do the work myself. There are the makings of a church there."

So we went to work with this small group of ten people. We started with two services a month here in this dining room, and very soon we had twenty-five or thirty people. We also organized a catechism, or more precisely what we call a Bible school, for children from six to twelve or thirteen years old. We grew fairly rapidly, for in three years we had meeting on Thursdays up to sixty children, using all the rooms in the house. We had to go to three services, and then four; we had sixty people in the dining room. It was bursting at the seams.

There was also a women's group. All this was done in seven or eight years, thanks to my wife's extraordinary work. I did the teaching, and she did what we call the *diaconie*, that is, the serving and visiting.

When did this take place?

We began in 1953. And in about 1960, we said to the church at Bordeaux: "Fifty families are now members and there are sixty children in the Bible school. Ten of them are preparing for their first communion. It is no longer possible for us to shoulder everything." The church agreed to buy a building right next door to us that happened to be unoccupied. And the men of the parish—not I, I am not at all a practical man—went to work to transform it into a church sanctuary.

It was an amazing experience. We had reached many families of laborers that were relatively poor. And in the beginning we said, "They will never dare to come here to the 'mansion.' " Now, the extraordinary thing is that we had for the most part the wives of laborers at the first women's meetings, and they came into this living room without being ill at ease. During these first years, the group could be described as having three unusual characteristics. First, the number of families who joined and the number who came regularly were practically identical; there were no "deadbeats" (people on the rolls but never in church). Next, those who joined came from the working classes, and unskilled laborers attended the service without any problem. Finally, there grew up among us a great bond of unity and friendship. Then everything changed when we had a sanctuary! The workingmen of the parish had made this room, working with all their hearts. When the room was finished and then inaugurated, it was over: we have hardly seen the workingmen again.

Did their wives also stop coming?

No, they have been much more faithful. But on the whole, when this building became the sanctuary, a sort of official church, those who had worked for it stopped coming.

What do you think is the explanation for this?

Basically, they were very happy to do physical work for the church. They had been coming here for four or five years; they knew us well; they rallied for this project; and then, when the chapel was opened, they felt less involved. They preferred being welcomed into a private home rather than into an official building. But when you resume a family setting, as we are doing now, people start coming again. If you have a parish meal on the church premises, there will be almost no one there. Have it in a home and there will be a crowd.

Are you still the pastor of this parish?

Not most of the time. Pastors have been assigned here. They haven't all succeeded. It's true that the role is a little difficult while I am still here. But right now everything is working fine and the present pastor is a real shepherd of the flock, as they say in the Protestant idiom.

How did you exercise the pastoral role?

For me, the pastor is both theologian and coordinator. I fall back once again into my old habit of beginning at the bottom. The pastor should not do things that others could do. Nor should he try to be everywhere. How many times have we seen fellowship meetings fail just because the pastor was there, making the meeting official by his presence? And it's true for me also, when I serve as pastor.

*You are in favor of very precise and distinct roles and
functions?*

In my opinion, the pastor has a role of preaching and
leading Bible study, of teaching, and also of relationship with the parish members through visiting. And
then he launches people into a particular work that
they must do themselves. For example, stimulating young
people so they form a young people's group does not
engage the pastor to participate in their meeting, nor in
meetings of women, the board of deacons, or others.
None of this is original. But what was original was that
with this work of preaching we actually reached the
people of the working class. Many refused to believe
this until they saw it with their own eyes. We knock
ourselves out trying to figure out how to reach the
working class; I know from experience: through a rigorous and simple preaching of the good news, but without
an ecclesiastical framework, without an organization or
a setting ready-made for them to fit into.

*Did you try to accomplish concretely on this small scale of
the parish what you were trying at the same time to accomplish through the committee on strategy?*

No, because there are few intellectuals here. Thus it is
almost impossible to stimulate a meditation on the
structures of society. However, it is possible to lead
someone to be more responsible in his profession, in
the group to which he belongs, and we experienced it.
During the worst moments of the war in Algeria and
the O.A.S.[1] we had meetings—not at my instigation

_____

1. A terrorist organization formed by several generals of the French

but at that of the pastor of that period—between Protestants whose opinions were resolutely opposed, and they were able to enter into dialogue. This can be done in a community of this kind. Much more than that isn't possible. But it's already a lot to be able to go beyond the most violent political disagreements.

In other respects, we are constantly faced with the question of how to bring the church to form a community. Above a certain number (around a hundred families) it is really impossible to have a sense of community: the parish should then be divided.

During the war in Algeria, did you think that Christians had something special to say, a prophetic message, a word from Christ?

The stand I took, which isolated me in the Reformed Church, consisted of refusing to take a side when people's hatred became implacable. There were several of us who, as early as the first war in Indochina, said that it was imperative to resolve the problem of colonization very, very quickly, to liberate the peoples of Africa and Asia very rapidly. Articles I wrote for *Réforme* and *Le Monde* can attest to my position.

Then, at the onset of the uprising—because at first it was only an uprising—several of us maintained that it was necessary to stop the repression immediately, agree to the modest demands of the F.L.N. [Algerian National Liberation Front] and resolve the problem politically: it was perfectly feasible. But very few Christians

---

army and politicians to subvert the policies of de Gaulle in Algeria.—TRANS.

were concerned about it. Then when there were killers on both sides, when the horrors of war were triggered—assassination attempts and torture—it was impossible to resolve the problem in the courts because the hatred between the two communities made it no longer possible to say who was right. Despite my conviction that it was necessary to end colonization, I could not simply take the side of the F.L.N. That was, unfortunately, too simplistic. I could not simply dismiss the presence . of more than a million French there who had developed the country. I was inevitably faced with the question: aren't these French people also in their homeland, settled there for a century or more? No one was ever able to answer the question I posed: "After how many years of occupation does one have the right to consider the land one's home?" For after all, the Arabs were also colonizers, invaders, a foreign occupation with respect to the Berbers and the Kabuls. So, because they were there for a thousand years, did they have more right than the French who were there for a hundred years? But after people began to take a stand based purely on emotion, no more reasonable questions could be posed. I stopped talking.

Christians had not pronounced a prophetic message when they should have: before the event, not after. In 1954 and 1955, no one listened to us. After that it was too late. We could only try to bind the wounds and prevent the hatred from growing. I don't believe that at that moment we should have taken a pro-war stand. That can only be done blindly out of emotion. When the war is started, no one is right any more. There is no more just cause. The just cause is spoiled; it becomes unjust by the means that are employed.

I criticize Christians for the fact that almost every time a concrete political question arises, they commit themselves after everyone else instead of seeing more clearly beforehand. What good is it, for example, to become a Marxist now? Christians should have been socialists seventy years ago. In our day when all of society has become more or less socialist, there is no more advantage to becoming a Marxist.

It is not a question of advantage but of belief.

What belief? The general belief. Everyone thinks in Marxist terms, consciously or unconsciously; the famous ruling class is socialist. That's not what I expect from Christians.

You want Christians to be ahead of tomorrow's history?

Exactly. And I want them to see how things are likely to develop so that they can intervene and prevent them from going in the worst direction.

Meanwhile, the war was there, and you did not take a side.

In regard to the war in Algeria, I was rather quickly led to take the same realistic position as at the time of the Munich treaty: either the government wants war, in which case it must totally crush Algeria; or else it has reservations, it doesn't entirely want war, it is not ready to crush a whole people; it must then make peace by liberating the Algerian people. Here is how I stated the problem one year after the first outbreak of rioting, when we escalated to a truly military involvement: you must know what you are doing when you start a war, and that's why you must not start one. But once you have started it, you can no longer have second thoughts.

War was there with all its horrors, and you said, "It's too late." In other words, when Christians proved themselves bad prophets, there was nothing left for them to do but to bury their heads in the sand.

Oh, no. I say the Christian should pick up the pieces, prepare for the postwar period, and begin immediately to work at reconciling people, at binding wounds, at considering how to cooperate with Algeria after the war. At that moment, taking sides meant the same as joining the army. I don't believe the Christian's role is to want a victor and a vanquished, no matter who they be.

Because for you, Christians are always one step ahead.

Unfortunately, they are always behind when they should be ahead. The Christian has a prophetic mission to try to think before events become inevitable. There are moments when history is flexible, and that is when we must put ourselves inside to move the works. But when the atomic bomb is dropped, it is no longer the moment to attach a parachute to it. It's all over. I don't believe in a permanent determinism, in the inexorable course of nature. Fate operates when people give up; when the structures of and the relationships between groups, special interests, coalitions, and ideologies are not yet rigid; when new facts appear that change the rules of the game; then at these moments we can make decisions that direct history, but very quickly everything becomes rigid and mechanical, and then nothing more can be done. One of my greatest disappointments is the extreme incapacity of Christians to intervene when situations are fluid and their habit of passionately taking sides when it is too late for anything but fate to operate. They are pushing the wheel of a vehicle that is already rolling downhill by itself.

8.

A New Training for Pastors

MADELEINE GARRIGOU-LAGRANGE: *When you make an assessment of your activities in the Church, it is hardly positive.*

JACQUES ELLUL: I would even say that it is not at all positive.

Was this the greatest failure in your life?

Certainly not. When a parish like this one, for example, happens to go downhill after having done very well, I say to myself: at one time, the people heard some truths here, they received a message from God, and that is very good. Why should it last for thirty-five

years? In the same way, I have good memories of all
that we undertook in the committee on strategy, of
what we created together there. At the time, it was
necessary to do it, just as later it was necessary to
intervene with the committee on theological studies.

I must add that when I said I had given up all
intervention at the top levels of the Reformed Church,
it was not quite exact. I had a definite role in these
reforms. We accomplished a real community effort
within a committee that functioned magnificently between 1969 and 1979.

How did you decide to undertake this new activity?

It really resulted from my disappointment and my failure in the national council. I had not started the Reformed Church in the direction of a new reform. Not
only that, but the council endlessly debated the subject
of the ministries necessary for the church. They made
lists that resulted in nothing. So I tried to imagine the
reform of the church from another angle, saying to
myself, "It isn't possible on the level of the church
members, but if we changed the training of pastors by
changing theological studies, the chances are that we
would have a new breed of pastors, ministers of the
church, diversified and inventive. And the life of the
church would change." This reasoning determined the
first project we started to develop with Jean Bosc in
1968.

Did you originate the idea of a reform of theological studies?

No, not at all. It was an idea that came up periodically. Since 1952 there had been countless projects, including a significant one by Pierre Maury. After reading them, with the help of Jean Bosc we wrote the first draft, which went much further than Jean Bosc had originally planned. We managed to finish developing this project in 1969.

What did your reform involve?

First, the plurality of ministries. Until then there was only one kind of training, that of pastor. A student entered the school of theology, he stayed there for three years, he spent a year as a pastor-in-training, and then he became a pastor. Once he was a pastor, he would become a writer, for example for *Réforme* magazine; or make television programs; or take charge of a parish, a school, a relief work, or a Christian organization; all of these with the same training, which did not seem the ideal situation to us!

The reform of theological studies was based on three main ideas. The first: it is not self-evident that theological studies must necessarily train church ministers. Why couldn't an individual study theology simply for its own sake? It thus seemed necessary to us to clearly distinguish two stages: first, a purely theological, academic, scientific, and intellectual program, for those who don't necessarily plan to become pastors. And then would come what we call the ministerial program, preparing for the ministry those who so desire. By this we hoped to discourage those who, at the age of eighteen, following the wishes of their families or out of religious sentimentality, enter a school of theology with the idea of becoming a pastor. I don't deny the calling of pastor, but I have seen so many failures along the way or disillusionment afterward that I think it would have been better to allow young people to think a little longer before committing themselves. In offering them an intellectual and practical education centered around theology but not at all "religious" and without spiritual emotionalism, we hoped to allow time for reflection. We also wanted to open this first program to adults and to non-Protestants, who would come there out of interest; for example, philosophy or history students who would be attracted to the school of theology for the subjects taught there.

And was this a success?

On the whole, yes. Almost half of the students in the academic program are not Protestants preparing for a pastoral ministry. We thought it would be equally advantageous if the young Protestants mingled with other students, instead of staying in a closed group as they did in the past. After this first cycle would then come a second one of two years duration, thus lengthening the course of study. It would be a ministerial program that would accept only those who, after reflection, truly wanted to exercise a ministry in the church. The training would then be given with emphasis on one of the possible ministries: preaching, practical theology, pastoring, ethics, and so on. And we hoped that as much as possible the students would, through training courses in charitable organizations, parishes, and various works of the church, choose a particular orientation and be trained for it instead of having only a theoretical knowledge of theology. Such was the first reform, already in itself upsetting the old order.

The second basic idea was that theology should develop connections with the social sciences. After all, in the twelfth and thirteenth centuries, theology and philosophy were compared; in the nineteenth and twentieth, theology and history; today we can no longer avoid making the connections between theology and psychology, sociology, economics, and political science. All the more so because pastors have shown a penchant for getting involved in politics, and they know nothing of it: it would be better to intellectually arm them for that. Thus, the training should include a strong social science education alongside the traditional theology courses.

The third guiding idea consisted of what has been termed the confrontation between theory and life. It is a response to two observations: first, there was the tendency of professors in their teaching to parrot the theology of the past instead of creating the theology needed for our times; next, pastors were extremely unprepared in the midst of the concrete problems that people of our day face, and this happened because they had never left the academic environment and had done nothing other than their studies. In answer to this dual concern, we instituted a system of training courses. Every year, each student would have to take a training course of four months in a business, in some kind of

company as an employee. Then after these four months
the students would return to the school, and there they
would have to review their training course; that is, the
students would make a sort of report on the questions
they encountered, their difficulties, their observations,
and so on. And this would be both compared with
reports by other students and studied by and with the
theology professors; that is, the latter would have to
consider from a theological standpoint the concrete
problems that anyone in the world faces. They could no
longer limit themselves to repeating what Calvin or
Luther said, because they said nothing on the situation
of the unskilled worker in the factory, or on the problems of transportation or of urban housing. Thus, the
students and professors would have to formulate a
theology centered around humanity's present condition and based on these experiences. Obviously, this
was a complete disruption of the status quo.

Besides these three principal axes, there was also a
series of less essential but still significant reforms: for
example, on the institutional level, a real participation
of students in the administration of the schools; the
school in Montpellier was run by the student body
representatives plus the faculty board. . . . In the same
vein, the penalties took the form of units of credit. In
addition, we envisioned a curriculum that would no
longer be decided by each professor according to his
interests but that was, rather, a thematic curriculum;
that is, one in which the professors would jointly choose
a theme for the year that would be the same for everyone and would be treated from all different angles by
the theologian, the ethics professor, the historian of

religions, the historian of the Reform, and so on. It was a pedagogical revolution.

Finally, we had two last ideas: since there were many subjects to cover, we would have added to the permanent teaching staff several temporary professors, calling on experts to come for short courses—six hours, for example. This would allow students to meet many of the best minds of our time. And one last thing: we feel the theological education is never finished, and after the transformation of theological studies, we had envisioned in a second stage starting up a continuing education program.

This represented a great upheaval of old habits. Did it work?

Yes and no. There was, of course, some very strong opposition from many theology professors and, in the ranks of the church, from all of the conservatives. However, the reform as a whole was accepted by the national synod in 1972, when I presented the project. From that point we began to apply it, which proved very difficult. For example, to be able to do everything, it would have been necessary to shorten the vacation period. There was a general outcry! Thus it was necessary to shorten the programs. In particular, the training courses were cut to three, then two months, leaving them with little importance. The review of training courses was poorly done; the theologians refused to have anything to do with this job. It was a battle of wills between the schools and the committee charged with implementing the reform.

Were you a member of this committee?

Of course. There were six of us.

And how did it operate? Did you go to the schools?

Yes, we went individually or as a group. We met with the professors and the students, who told of the difficulties, the refusals, and the lapses; and we searched for answers. And each year we made a report on the progress and the setbacks and on the changes to be made.

And you were in agreement within this committee?

It was a great joy to me that the six members of the committee formed a small but real community of minds and lives.

You came from different theological backgrounds?

Of course. There were two Lutherans and four Reformed, of which two could be called conservative and two of modern tendency.

But after all was said and done, after so much effort, don't we see today a retreat from this reform?

There is no doubt that the second program at Montpellier works quite well and pastors who were trained along the lines of our project are of excellent quality. But, in spite of everything, the major changes are being trimmed away little by little, the continuing education was never begun, the training courses are on the shelf, the thematic and interdisciplinary curriculum has practically been abandoned, and the education in social sciences is almost nil. In 1977, after four years of effort, we truly believed it would succeed, but we have seen for the past three years a kind of retreat. And yet I remain convinced that this reform was the opportunity for the Reformed Church to reform itself and, furthermore, to demonstrate the actual invention of a new academic model. Too bad . . . As Romain Gary said in *Tulipe*, "Another patrol screwed up!" But it's not over yet. New professors could revive the project.

9.

With the Street Gangs

MADELEINE GARRIGOU-LAGRANGE: *At the same time you were on the council of the Reformed Church, you carried on right here in Pessac a very different kind of activity with street gangs. How did you, a scholar and theologian, in sum, a highly respected man, become interested in young dropouts?*

JACQUES ELLUL: It happened in an unusual way. One day a young Protestant girl came to me, saying, "I know a counselor working with juvenile delinquents who could use some legal advice." I replied, "I'm not a lawyer, but if it isn't too difficult . . ." And I received a visit from an amazing young man, Yves Charrier. He told me, "I am a counselor at the Prado, but for several months I have been trying to make contact with the street gangs. If I know of a crime and I don't turn in the culprit, what could happen to me?" "That's very simple," I replied. "You are an accomplice."

"Hmm. That's very annoying. You see, if I turn him in, it's all over with, I can no longer do anything at all with them because no teenager will trust me any more." And he explained to me what he planned to do. "Rehabilitation in a closed environment is fine while the youth is in an institution, but all you have accomplished falls apart as soon as he gets back to his natural environment. I think we have to work with unconfined teenagers in their own environment; if they develop in a positive direction there, they won't fall back again."

While remaining at the Prado to earn a living, Charrier thus went to work in the streets, and I was a kind of safety net for him. First, he needed me because he felt isolated in undertaking this work of prevention, which was completely unheard-of in 1957–58; he had to think out the actions he should take, and I served as his complement. Little by little, I learned to work with this element that was called the "black jackets" in those days. And then, for the second factor, you were right to describe me as a respected man in my field, and as such, I could answer for Yves Charrier in the event that his work led him into difficulties with the police or the district attorney's office. I then intervened to explain what kind of work he was doing.

Did his work involve violence?

Charrier was an athlete, a strong man, and we were in the era of the black jackets. One day he told me, "There are guys that need one good beating to start a positive relationship." We talked about it for a long time and I finally responded, "Yes, that is probably true, but on the condition that you don't do it in the heat of anger, but only after thinking about it." After that, every time Charrier felt it was necessary to start a fight and teach someone a lesson, he came to talk it over with me, and when we concluded that, in fact, a guy only had influence on the others (for instance, leading them into delinquent acts) because of his physical reputation, then Charrier would provoke a fight and rough him up. It happened fairly often.

Did this take place in public, in front of his buddies?

Always; and afterward, Charrier reported to me, "His face was black and blue, but I didn't hurt him too much. For the next five days his buddies will see that he got demolished but that I didn't knock him out."

He was an extraordinary young man. He was gifted with his hands—he had started as a cabinetmaker—and he was also intuitive, he sensed every situation. He liked working in tandem with me, saying, "I don't have faith—you have it for me."

He was not a tender man, he was hard. But he did have a motivating faith. Although he had never read the Gospel, one day when he was in anguish over a youth who seemed to have no future, he said to me, "I can't bear for one of these little ones to be lost."

You didn't have direct contact with these street gangs?

Not until the existence of the club. I was too old, and that work requires one to be very athletic and strong. Also, it was very unofficial until a judge, Monsieur Martaguet, became interested in it and got the minister of justice to pay a salary to Charrier so he could devote himself entirely to this work.

It was in 1958, and this was the first work of prevention in the province of Bordeaux; there were only two or three in France at the time. We organized a club, recruited a staff, and Charrier and I established what we called "the philosophy of prevention." We said that prevention could not consist in adapting young people to society. Twenty years ago this was hard to put over; the common conception of this kind of work was very simple: the youths who stole should stop stealing, those who drank should stop drinking, and those who didn't work should go to work. We said, "No, that's not the problem." Besides, we weren't dealing with predelinquents but with young dropouts who were basically unhappy. What struck us the most, under their shell of brutality, was actually their poverty. Not primarily their economic poverty, but their intellectual poverty: we observed that they had about a hundred and twenty words in their vocabulary, the rest consisting of interjections. And they had an emotional poverty, poverty in their relationships. They were truly unhappy.

Also, nothing interested them. Many of them, by the way, did not come from poor families but from the middle class. What they lacked most were relationships. They were bored everywhere. Their stock phrase was, "What a drag." A kid becomes delinquent just starting with that. What could they really do? Steal? It's fun to steal, it procures a feeling of power. Stealing cars, causing accidents, playing with weapons, threatening to kill yourself, attacking a guy because you don't like the way he looks—all this for no reason.

It was for the act itself.

Exactly. For example, stealing didn't really have theft as a motive. But going into other people's houses to sack the place, break the mirrors, eat and drink what is in the fridge, sleep in the owners' beds—that is exciting! A sort of rape and sacrilege. For a moment they are the bosses, and they laugh at it all.

Now, it was possible to have an influence on these boys, who in those days were hard, active, and athletic. All you had to say was, "If you want to be strong like so-and-so, you shouldn't drink." It was dumb, but it worked every time.

Because they were active, Charrier decided that they needed to have activities suggested to them. And the club was organized for this purpose: scuba diving, sky diving, cave exploration, canoeing and kayaking, and then machine, metal, and wood shops. It was at the beginning of the electric guitar fad. Charrier learned the technique and told them, "You can't buy them, they're too expensive, so you're going to make them." The same thing for the diving equipment: an expert came to the club; we bought the raw materials and the tools, and the guys made their diving equipment.

Were there girls too?

Everything was coed, of course. But in these gangs of boys, the girls were with few exceptions only auxiliary, contemptible objects. We said to ourselves, what can we do to keep them from being considered worthless? And we had an idea that will seem outdated to you in light of the present feminist discourse. The boys' power was in their physical strength. The girls' power over these boys could and should be their capacity to charm, or possibly their beauty. Now, they were terribly dressed, like the crassest streetwalkers. At the club we opened an area that was off limits to the boys, where the girls were at home—what a revolution—and it was not easy to enforce this discipline. We opened a beauty salon where a beautician taught these girls simply how to wash their hair, to be clean, to put on makeup. This was a means of education because it forced the boys to think of the girls—shall we say—as living beings. It was a great success.

Later the girls' section was developed: for example, a home economics teacher came to give cooking classes. We started a cooking club, and since we often had guys who were down and out eating at the club, the girls' standing was very much enhanced by their good cooking. But make no mistake, we had no intention of preparing them to be good little housewives! The only goal was to permit them to find a specific identity in confronting these boys and no longer let themselves be manipulated by them.

There must have been a whole team of specialists to operate the club.

We had to form an association; to find money, because all this was costly; to recruit a technical staff comprising a juvenile judge, a sociologist, a psychologist, a psychiatrist, and a psychoanalyst. Once a month, the staff of counselors came to discuss their problems, and we worked together to find educational ideas. It all worked very well, but we often had experiences that horrified people. Here is a typical one: Charrier said one day, very annoyed, "Weapons have shown up at the club— paratrooper knives and even a gun. What should we do?" After long consideration, the team decided that there would be no question of taking the weapons away from these very insecure boys. It would be better to give them confidence. And at the first opportunity, when one of them cut himself above the kneecap in acting like a fool with his knife, Charrier said to them, "Look, you aren't even capable of using a knife. What if someone taught you how?" And they were taught how to throw a paratrooper knife. When people heard about that, they said we were crazy: "These armed hooligans will be dangerous." For three months, there was knife fever at the club. And then, when the youths really knew how to use them, the weapons disappeared.

Were you accused of creating, with the club, a place where stolen goods were exchanged?

Yes, of course, and we heard all possible accusations periodically. But after numerous conflicts, we managed little by little to make two successive police commissioners understand our point of view, so that before they took any action against one of the youths of the club, they telephoned me first, saying, "So-and-so just did this damn fool thing. We know he is one of Charrier's boys. What do you think about it?"

And you as a university professor and respected citizen answered for them?

You could say I answered for some illegal acts, offenses, and violations. It is obvious that a prevention counselor in the open setting knows about these delinquent activities: he is inevitably on both sides of the fence at the same time. For example, at the time when nobody in France (long before 1968) talked about drug abuse, Yves Charrier had observed extensive use of it among young people. We organized an informative meeting with specialists who would have competence in fields touching on drug abuse (doctors, teachers, police detectives), and Yves explained what he had observed. An eminent representative of the police disagreed violently with him, asserting, "Drugs do not exist in Bordeaux." "You want some? Here," Yves answered, taking from his pockets some small packages. "This is some marijuana, this is cocaine, these are amphetamines. All these were handed over to me by the guys."

I saw a lot of these "maladjusted kids" as they called them then. I went to the club often in the evening and almost every Sunday afternoon.

Did you talk to them?

There wasn't very much we could talk about. We were there, we joked around. By the way, a lot of other young people—well intentioned, especially some Christians—wanted to get involved. They came to the club and were terribly disappointed. "It's ridiculous," they told me. "The music is so loud you can't talk." I answered, "Yes, but you don't realize the importance of your presence; by the very fact that you are there they have an alternative model to their own environment."

A model that can't be imitated. Isn't that depressing?

You know, they never had an image of me as an impossible model. Seeing that I wasted my time with them, they saw me as a normal adult, a good guy. I don't know how many times I heard this complaint when they talked of their parents: "I never see them. They don't have time. I see my father on Saturday and he asks me, 'You have your cash?' That's all he says to me all week."

Even if it wasn't your goal, didn't the club contribute to bringing these young people back into society?

The goal was not, I repeat, to make them fit in, but rather to help them develop, by their own means and in their own environment, a personality that would permit them to go beyond their conflicts. Whether or not they adopted a political orientation, whether or not they continued in delinquence, did not bother us. The most important thing was that they become adults able to take responsibility for themselves and that they discover something exciting for their lives. No matter what; some of them became interested in sculpture, others in photography.

You didn't make plans for their future?

None whatsoever. And we didn't try to direct them toward a profession. On the other hand, when we saw a guy panic—"I don't have a trade, what's going to happen to me?"—we tried at all costs to find a career prospect for him.

This is the kind of work we did up until Charrier's death. He died in 1969 while scuba diving.

Did you leave the club then?

Oh, not at all! On the contrary, after this happened, the counseling team was at a low point, and because I thought this work was essential for the young people, I said to myself, "We absolutely must hang on." And for a year's time I filled the role of team leader, reorganizing all the work. Quite obviously we needed a leader. And the great difficulty was that the team could only think of prevention along the lines of one model, that of Charrier.

Now, for two years previously the clientele of the club had been changing greatly. As forthright, tough, and athletic as he was, Charrier was as bad at handling these inactive, gentle kids as he was good at handling the black jackets, motorcyclists, and thieves. "So-and-so has only one goal in life," he told me. "He has discovered an uninhabited cave, moved in, and doesn't set foot outside. Four chicks bring him his grub. His ideal is not to do a damn thing. What can I possibly do with a guy like that?" he concluded. The model of prevention that we had for the club was not at all suited to this new generation. It took me three years before I found a new counselor the caliber of Charrier, while being almost his opposite. He is strong, too, and could use his fists. But for some admirable personal reasons he refuses to use the slightest bit of force. He is a man of dialogue and of human relationships. And he is the man needed for these lost young people on drugs. They are just as maladjusted but much more sophisticated than the primitive brutes Charrier was dealing with.

Did you continue going to the club?

There was no more club. Luc Fauconnet closed it. And the team of counselors, which was also completely replaced, works only in the streets. The work is much more vague, based essentially on the personal relation. For from the moment a human relation comes into existence, a transition or a development becomes possible.

It is a dialogue between two people.

Yes, but the team meets once a week to pool their experiences. And I will also mention that we have always focused our prevention in Pessac on the hardest ones, the most extreme dropouts, believing that it means nothing to bring back to normal a little flock of very nice young people, because this flock will inevitably be attracted to a leader, and this leader will be the toughest one. That is one of the disagreements between the team (and the association) at Pessac and many other prevention teams who prefer to work with very young people that haven't yet gone over to the other side. They are then doing a kind of boy scouting. We have always refused to do that here.

So you still have approximately the same role you had before?

No, because in the self-managed team of counselors that Fauconnet prefers, the study group has much less importance. Also, the preventive work is criticized by everyone right now: by the police, by the public, and by the government, who pay a lot for it and get nothing in return. Thus, my position is no longer one of providing legal protection but of winning acceptance for the work of prevention. I spent time starting a federation of clubs for prevention in the Gironde region. This took several years. Then, knowing that the minister of health had a project centralizing everything, we thought it was absolutely necessary for the associations of prevention to join together on the national level to defend the specific nature of prevention. After many years and difficulties, we succeeded in creating the National Committee for Unity between Clubs and Teams of Prevention.

Your role was that of theorist?

I am a little like a grandfather to it.

The charismatic personality?

You could put it that way. When it was all finished, Fauconnet encouraged me to step down, saying, "You have done enough in the last twenty years." I thus withdrew; the team is working well, the association is working well, and I'm happy. I remain a kind of resource. Sometimes they even call on me again for help.

How do you explain the fact that you were motivated so intensely and for so long in this activity?

I told you. I was led into it by accident, my chance meeting with Charrier. In an hour we were friends.

The fact that the man's character and actions were somewhat outside of society's norms undoubtedly had an influence on you.

Yes, this kind of action was very suited to me, of course. I was equally struck by a dimension of Christian authenticity. It wasn't possible for me as a Christian to remain indifferent to the unhappiness of these young people. And there was a third factor, this one theoretical: my analysis of technical society shows that, by its strict organization and functioning, it pushes more and more people to the sidelines of society. All those who do not conform to the level of efficiency society demands are pushed aside.

Then I found myself confronted with young people exactly like those I had described in my articles showing how technical efficiency excludes groups. In helping

these young people become well balanced and complete human beings, albeit misfits with regard to technical development, I was in a sense taking a stand
against technical society.

*Have you ever thought that these misfits could be in a way
the heralds of a different society or, shall we say, a parallel
society?*

They seemed to me, and still do, so fragile, so scared to
death to enter this life and fail to measure up. "A
profession is hard," they say. "You have to be smart to
do that. I'm not smart." They are also very unhappy. A
positive or negative word can completely change things.
   That's why I wouldn't say they can be the basis for
a new society. It is certain, however, that they are the
sign that our society cannot continue as it is. But I don't
think a project for society can be founded with them as a
starting point. They don't represent what the working
class represented for Marx. One of Marcuse's mistakes
was counting on these young misfits to produce a
revolution.

*Even without a project, doesn't the influence you have on
such fragile beings constitute a project in itself? Aren't they
motivated to follow the counselor-leader who opens himself to
them?*

That's precisely the amazing work of a man like Fauconnet, who forces them, not to follow, but to find their
own place. It is a process of teaching that grows as the
young person's capacity to accept it grows. The coun-

selors who are really doing this are working themselves to death. After having met many counselors, I only know two categories of them worthy of the name: the Christians and the communists. One must have profound motives for doing this work.

What impact did 1968 have on the young people and the counselors?

On the young people, none at all. The majority of them couldn't care less about politics. They didn't understand at all what happened. However, it seemed to the counselors—it is the subject of a great debate in the field of prevention—that there was in 1968 a fundamental transformation of society that means there will be no more misfits. This was not the hope of all the counselors, but it was for a great number.

And did you agree with them?

Absolutely not. I am convinced that in any organized society some groups in the population are pushed aside; the very fact of social life pushes people out, some more than others.

And in your opinion, technical society has a particularly great power to push people out.

Yes, but a radically different choice of society should arise through the ecologists and other similar trends. The dream of the counselors was not this at all: many of the numerous extreme left-wing counselors put their hopes in a communist society. No matter how much we told them that in the USSR there are a large number of misfit groups entirely akin to ours, they couldn't believe it. Now, it's a fact that the communist society pushes people out more than any other society. The number of those excluded is beyond imagination.

Did your activity with young dropouts change some of your ideas?

Of course. I don't believe it changed my sociological analysis of society. But it certainly pushed me toward a greater theological openness and toward a greater compassion in my preaching.

I should mention that during the club's existence I led Bible study groups. Charrier came to me saying, "There are four or five of them who are asking religious questions. Would you come talk to them?" It was out of the question to speak in religious language to them and bring them into a closed world; I had to create good, biblically authentic theology that could be immediately understood. This required a stripping of vocabulary and a sharpening of the intellect. These groups made me work hard and had a great influence on me.

Did you change your interpretation of the Bible on the subject of violence, both individual and social violence?

I became much more sensitive to social violence than to the individual violence of young people. The phenomenon of social violence—administrative violence, violence of the judicial system, and so on—has been for me the frightening discovery of something against which we are totally helpless. Very recently, Fauconnet was in torment over a boy he had worked with for four years. On strong drugs, arrested several times for burglaries, he had little by little given up drugs and had realized that his life up to that point had been meaningless. He had met a girl, got married, found a job; he is very intelligent and did very well. And then, the other day, the police came to his place of work with a warrant to interrogate, and took him away. He protested, "I haven't done anything for over a year." They answered that it was for a simple matter of questioning. At the station, the detective affirmed that he was only there for a minor traffic violation, but then he recalled that the boy owed some legal fees for an old case. "I have a good job," the boy said. "I can pay them right away." "No," said the detective, "you'll stay in jail and pay tomorrow." The next day another detective who had known him before handcuffed him and took him to his place of work where everyone could see him that way; they took a search warrant to his house and tore it apart in front of his wife. They found absolutely nothing against him. But he lost his job.

There is a basic inhumanity in this treatment. You could say that procedures like the example I just gave you are based on the belief that someone who has committed an offense can never again become a different person. Now, all our work of prevention is based on exactly the opposite belief (and coincides here with Christianity). That is why I always explain to the police that prevention and repression are not compatible. We are relying on the conviction that there remains a possibility of change. And, happily, we know kids who used drugs and have given them up.

*This conviction is in keeping with your belief that all people
are saved.*

There is a link between them, of course. But, based on
my involvement in all this, I thus have to renounce the
idea that to be saved it is sufficient to do good. Of the
young people I encountered, I can't say there was no
good in them, but they were characterized above all by
their fragility and their unhappiness. When Jesus draws
near to these little ones, it is not because of the potential for good in them, it is because they are unhappy.

To me, they are not latent Christians, although
some of them have become Christians. They are also
not Christians without knowing it. But I am convinced
that they too have a place in God's love.

This experience of prevention had a marked influence on me, and it also permitted me to realize that all
the government agencies are not of the same cloth,
producing the same social violence; there are some
people who are more open than others, and one can
work with that.

*Do you think that technical society can adopt measures that
will allow it to be less violent or, if that doesn't work, create
areas where violence is less used?*

It's true that the temptation will exist to reserve such
areas, to create Indian reservations. Society could
function very well with several hundred or several
thousand outcasts that would never be seen. But, inasmuch as their number would likely grow, the process
of development itself would be called into question. I

say this without being absolutely convinced of it. I have seen so many of these students who were violent protesters in 1968 become, two years later, admirable conformists.

But there are also these general movements that are cropping up all over, and they have a completely different approach. I think of the ecologists (but there are such conflicts and diversity among them), the non-violence advocates, the movements of scientists who question science, those who resist in their jobs, the Catholic study groups in various professions, the charismatic communities, and women! They are all looking for another way, outside of political means. They are signs of the inevitable upheaval that is going to take place. Nevertheless, I still don't believe this will bring about a profound change in technical society.

You might as well say that technical society has a good future ahead.

Unless it grinds to a halt by itself, if it provokes chaos within itself, which is very possible. The further I go, the more I am convinced that there will be points of breakdown. It's absolutely certain, and these groups are the sign.

They will blow everything apart?

Certainly not, but they will prevent a good number of technical mechanisms from operating. It is important to note that in the domain of energy, no one knows any more what should be done. In addition, one part of the opinion has changed. We have said a thousand times, Charbonneau and I, that the first step would be the awakening to one phenomenon or another. Now this awakening that I didn't believe would come is happening little by little.

You seem to think that small actions that succeed or fail are still blows to society that to some degree disturb it.

Not by themselves, no, because our society has extraordinary strength and ability to recover, but what is happening is like a gnawing away by termites. And we can't forget that the more strong, organized, rapid, and complete a society is, the more fragile it is, unable to tolerate a grain of sand. We are doing nothing other than putting in grains of sand. But we must keep in mind that it is a matter of changing principles and plans in this society, and not a simple political change; consequently, it is a much slower process, and is more difficult to evaluate. This describes the problem with the coast of Aquitaine, which we can take up in a minute.

But it could also be said, in the area of youth and prevention, that even without bringing a young person to a point of intellectual awareness, every time we can lead him to take responsibility for his life and go beyond his problems, it is a victory over the technical system. Every time an individual actually becomes an adult, it is a victory over the technical system. I am absolutely certain of this. Even if our work with a few people was amateur compared to the system's enormous kneading of the masses, this work is qualitatively more significant. Besides, I feel that even if the system does not change, we must help young people who right now suffer with this condition of fragility, the misfits I described a few minutes ago. This doesn't mean that it isn't also necessary to work to change the social system. But the work of the craftsman and the amateur on the individual level seem very important to me.

One last thing. Among the young people you met at the club, haven't some of them become adults who have actually joined the system?

To some extent, yes. The guy who gets married, becomes happy, finds work he is suited to that allows him to remain in control of his life—I don't know if he has joined the system; at any rate, he has become a responsible man. In appearance he's not very different from many others, but their adventures give all those I have known a special human force. Some of them have a role like that of the shepherds of Giono,[1] those men of experience and wisdom who are able to help and counsel.

They didn't need a psychologist or psychiatrist?

Never, or almost never. They had human companionship, an unselfish friend they knew they could count on. This is essential. Qualitative change can only take place by re-establishing the human relation, without ulterior motives, without moralizing, accepting the

---

1. French writer of the twentieth century who celebrated, among other things, the pastoral life. —TRANS.

other without judging. This friendship is the most radical attack that can be made on either a technical society dedicated to efficiency or on a communist society based on conformity and informing on others. And it is what makes real prevention so radical.

10.

A Fascinating and Terrifying World

MADELEINE GARRIGOU-LAGRANGE: *For years you have fought against M. I. A. C. A., the interdepartmental mission to ameliorate the coast of Aquitaine. How did you come to carry the environmentalist banner like this?*

JACQUES ELLUL: It was after a long path of study that, besides, was more Charbonneau's than mine. Whereas I drew the motivations of my actions from the revelation, he found his in his extraordinary passion for nature.

A lifelong passion?

Yes. I was thoroughly a city boy, and he lived only when he left the city. He taught me to know the forest and the mountains, but not the sea—the sea is something quite different. He took me to these places and made me love them.

You who call yourself a city boy have made the city a terrifying universe in your books.

I saw it as a world both fascinating and terrifying at the same time. When I was young it was my holy place—attractive and fearsome. I see in the city a creation by man separated from God by his own decision.

Didn't God himself give the world to human beings, telling them, "Create it"?

I believe God never told man to recreate the world, and the concept of a creation completed by man, perfected and exploited by him, is entirely false. God told man in Genesis to rule, to subjugate, to fill the creation that is made for him, of which he is the head, the ruler, but nothing more. And this took place before what is fallaciously termed the Fall (in imitation of other myths) and what is in reality man's separating himself from God.

Before or after, what does it matter?

It's not at all the same thing. In the Genesis account man is in perfect communion with God, his opposite.

The command, "Subjugate nature," calls man to subjugate it as God subjugates man: solely by love, for we must always come back to this essential point, that God *rules by love and not by strength.*

From the moment man broke with God and took his independence, and God let him do it, the relationship of things changed in every aspect. Man became a master over nature, which is actually delivered over to him. If you compare the account of Noah's covenant with that of creation, the great distance between the two accounts will be apparent to you. From then on, "nature will fear you and dread you." If you compare the two accounts of covenants (Genesis 1:29–30 and Genesis 9:2–7), you find the same expressions, with more or less two exceptions: in the covenant with Noah, God adds, "You will be feared and dreaded by every beast of the earth . . . by every creature that lives on the earth; they are delivered into your hand. . . . Every living thing shall be food for you." This has thus nothing in common with the covenant of peace and communion that we find in Genesis 1. In other words, in the creation covenant, Adam rules by love and also by the spoken word, since the animals pass before him to be named. He thus exercises an intellectual authority over the natural world. After the Fall, Noah's covenant allows mankind one thing that was excluded from the first covenant: they may kill and eat animals, and they will ever after rule by fear. With the separation, everything changed.

The Golden Age came to an end?

It's not at all the equivalent of a golden age, because the latter is always centered around human happiness, whereas the vision of creation is one of universal communion.

Is it a world without tensions or conflicts?

Of course. It is a world of communion and unity.

Even though the separation brings conflict, I don't see why it would take away from man his creative calling.

But before the separation he was in communion with God; thus we might say he participated in creation, in the sense that creation is not a static object, dead and cast aside. It is always in the process of being renewed, always alive like love itself. And man brought God's love into this creation, thus making it truly live and change. But from the moment this separation exists, man makes creation his object, a world in his image, a world of separation, of conflict, of disorder. Of course, he remains the ruler of creation, and that is why Romans 8—"creation groans and suffers"—has had such importance for me. But man becomes an inexorable master, and instead of helping creation to develop fully, he exploits it tragically, incoherently, until it is used up.

What in your opinion can man do after the separation with nature? That is the concrete question you face in the matter of the coast of Aquitaine.

The Bible says, "The earth will bear thorns and this-
tles for you." It announces that man and nature are ever
after hostile to each other. On this point Charbonneau
and I obviously did not see eye to eye. Doubtless he
never would say that nature was virgin or original, so to
speak. He always asserted that, on the contrary, the
nature we know is a product of man's work. When we
walk in the Landes forest, it seems extremely wild to us,
but it was planted by men, it is their creation and a
recent one. So the nature we know appears original but
has really been worked and reworked. But Charbonneau
has always thought that there exists an irreplaceable
relation between this so-called natural environment and
man. His love and his concern for nature led him to the
now popular concept that "one cannot pursue infinite
development within a finite world"; Charbonneau said it
in 1944. At that time, this inspired understanding didn't
strike me. I wasn't at all an environmentalist.

Despite all you had said already on the dangers of Technique?

Technique seemed terribly dangerous to Charbonneau
because it threatened nature and man in nature. It was
dangerous to me insofar as it threatened man's ability to
hear the Word of God. We complemented each other
well, our two arguments combining to make one fairly
complete one, but our references were different.

Around 1945 or 1946, when he lamented the destruction of a forest to build houses, I told him: "What do
you want? People really need houses now." The tangi-
ble needs of people seemed to me to take precedence

over those of the natural environment. Charbonneau, while being an amazing intellectual, always
had a much stronger sensory experience than I. Even
so, he had foreseen that every time nature is called into
question, man in his whole being is inevitably called
into question also.

After a period in which this orientation toward the
natural environment was relatively unimportant in our
experiences, it became more and more important,
starting with the moment we saw it strongly attacked.
But, much more important, we tried to express this
commitment in a concrete, timely application. We
were given the opportunity with the appearance of the
interdepartmental mission for development of the coast
of Aquitaine.

*So this was your first environmental battle. And you fought
it together with your friend?*

Charbonneau was the first to see it all coming. I joined
him right away and we fought together.

When did it begin?

Right after Phillipe Saint-Marc was evicted, when there
was a festival at Bordeaux to inaugurate the Aquitaine
mission. I wouldn't say we were favorable before that,
but there were committees composed of geographers,
ecologists, sociologists, all sorts of experts who studied
the possible development. Their purpose already was
actually to exploit the Aquitaine region, but these
experts seriously studied each situation and warned, "If

you do this, here is what disaster will result to the Landes forest; if you develop in that direction, such-and-such a trade that still exists will disappear."

They were advocates for the status quo?

They encouraged a prudent, reasonable development that would take into account local limitations. As for me, I was pretty favorable to the Saint-Marc project. Charbonneau was more critical. "Saint-Marc is right in wanting to save the Leyre valley," he said, "but through attracting everyone's attention to it, he will cause an influx of tourists and this heavy concentration of people will ruin the region."

Obviously, the Saint-Marc project was much more complicated, more reasonable and respectful of the natural setting than the project later conceived by Biasini and the Aquitaine mission. When we saw that to launch this project there would be a festival week with a great display of songfests and other activities, we spontaneously organized an antifestival week that eventually was reduced to one evening, but we attracted an incredible number of people.

You were one of its organizers?

No, it was Charbonneau and a small group, including particularly several militants of the P.S.U. [Unified Socialist Party]. I was invited. There were speakers and folksongs in Provençal all on the theme: "Defend the coast of Aquitaine; don't let them sell or auction off our region."

A committee was established. Their objectives were to find out the projects of M.I.A.C.A.—that was very difficult—and then to study them. But the major difficulty was this: one of our criticisms of M.I.A.C.A. was its centralizing methods. They made plans, decided on them, and applied them, without ever consulting the opinions of the populations concerned. (At best, they obtained an agreement from the city governments; we'll come back to that.) In our defense committee we wanted precisely to avoid the same technocratic methods, that is, creating counterprojects from above. From then on, our first preoccupation was to alert the people, the grass roots, about M.I.A.C.A.'s projects. We wanted to cause people to think about them, study them, and form local groups that would take the initiative. This was the only way for us to act in honesty.

And is that what really resulted?

Yes, the action only succeeded in areas where groups formed by local inhabitants existed. If we couldn't mobilize them, they weren't very strong. Local committees were created all over, at Verdon, at Hourtin, at Arcachon, in the Basque region, and later at Soulac, at Lacanau—

And those of you from Bordeaux, the intellectuals, what did you do with these grass-roots volunteers?

We gave them the research and arguments; we held public meetings; and when they informed us of something that didn't seem legal, we took legal action. In short, we put ourselves at the service of those who took matters in hand locally. But at the outset these people were often motivated by personal interests. One owned a small villa on the beach, and he learned that a building was going to be constructed right in front of his villa; another had made a campground and then discovered that there was a project for a marina on his land. We had an educational job to do, telling them: your interest is legitimate, but you can only be on the committee if you become a center of resistance and you assemble people to defend the interests of the group, the town, and the whole coast. Most of them joined with this perspective. One of our successes was in bringing them beyond a personal reaction to a communal debate. They ended up fighting collectively. It was very impressive.

But of course we encountered all sorts of obstacles. First, the conflicts between local groups: for example, it was incredibly hard to convince the three unions of oyster farmers of the Bassin d'Arcachon to fight together. We explained to them that, at any rate, if the projects of M.I.A.C.A. were accomplished, there would be no more oyster farming.

Then there was the skepticism of the communities. After a meeting at Lacanau, the people told us, "There's no reason to panic. We know how slow the government is. We'll see about it twenty years from now. We'll all be dead before they start." They didn't panic until the bulldozers arrived to level the sand dunes. But then it was too late.

A third obstacle came from the city governments. Some of them were literally blinded by the thought of the money all this would bring in. There would be three times as many tourists; local taxes would disappear; it was wonderful. The small businessmen, too, were sure that the influx of tourists would bring them rivers of money.

And of course the Aquitaine mission did what it could to influence the public. During vacation months, the mission sent groups of organizers to the beaches to convince people to support their projects. I might add that they generally failed in this direct contact with the public. But they were for a time successful with city governments and even more so with several politicians and journalists, thanks to an excellent program of public relations. For years we were unable to have articles published in certain newspapers, particularly *The Sud-Ouest.* They only had articles in favor of the Aquitaine mission. We were seriously hindered by the monopoly of news in the region.

What were your criticisms of M.I.A.C.A.?

First, the central idea itself seemed wrong to us: that Aquitaine is a poor region. It has as capital the sea, the forest, and the lakes. This capital is unexploited. It must be made to produce, that is, an enormous tourism project must be implemented. Tourism will enrich the region and will be its source of income. Thus, it was first this idea of exploiting a region that set us against them. But of course M.I.A.C.A. responded to this with a reassuring argument: they had to act to "protect nature" at the same time as they developed the region.

They didn't see that these two orientations are contradictory: how can you protect nature when you bring ten or twenty thousand more tourists into an area, with the inevitable ports, marinas, highways, and stores?

And in this situation, what did you do?

We attacked on three levels:

First, on the level of legal operations, some of which were patently irregular. We filed several suits that, I will add, we lost. I must say that it was a great disappointment for me. The administrative courts used to be truly independent from the government and able to make legal judgments. In this M.I.A.C.A. affair, the administrative courts were outrageous, judging in favor of the government when there were obvious irregularities. And a government representative even told us privately, "I totally agree with you, but I cannot act in any other way." If the administrative courts had acted properly, M.I.A.C.A.'s activities would have been greatly hampered. But of course this kind of battle is expensive for an association like ours, without income, and it can only be conducted by experts.

Second, we attacked on the technical level. We did very serious and thorough studies of the various M.I.A.C.A. projects and often discovered stupid, monumental mistakes. I will just mention one example: the trans-Aquitaine canal that was to connect the lakes between Hourtin and Bayonne, crossing the Bassin d'Arcachon. They began digging without even realizing that the lakes being connected are not at the same elevation, so that one empties into another. After finishing the first section, they had to fill the canal back up as quickly as possible!

Supposing that M.I.A.C.A. had had excellent technicians who designed a perfect canal, your opposition would have been the same.

If they had had very good technicians in all the fields, their projects would not have been the same. A good technician would never have thought that you could put seven thousand more boats on the Bassin d'Arcachon, because it is quite simply impossible. There were enormous material errors, such as the construction of a seawall at the entry to Capbreton; it completely changed the ocean currents. All the seamen of the region said that at the first storm coinciding with a spring tide, the seawall would be ruined. Two years later, it collapsed. All of this was not serious but cost millions of francs.

Third, we challenged, on a more or less economic level, the policy of ignoring the interests of local populations and the needs of the natural environment. Whereas the mission promised an increase in revenues, the small businessmen ended up losing money because the construction of marinas and luxury buildings led to the construction of a shopping center. On their part, the city governments contracted heavy debts because they had to help finance the support systems. And they quickly had to raise taxes. At Lacanau, taxes quadrupled in two years and the new city government refused to finish the third part of the planned construction.

They complain, but a little later you can't take it away from them.

The myth has a long life. In the past several years, some economic studies have begun to surface that say: if you take into account all investments, tourism definitely brings ready cash that circulates, but it doesn't benefit the local population. At the Bassin d'Arcachon, it can be easily seen that the local permanent trades, oyster farming, for example, threaten to disappear. In exchange for what? An influx of tourists for two months during which the inhabitants become café waiters and hotel maids. This is not development.

What exactly are you contesting: the creation of a tourist region, or a certain kind of tourism practice? People have vacations, and they have to go somewhere. Some of them have second residences, but others don't.

We contest the style of vacation of the guy who goes to the mountains or the seaside, goes skiing or motorboating for two weeks, and then leaves. This is a really detestable kind of vacationing and tourism. On the other hand, it seems important that the French discover not only the sea and the mountains, but also all the regions, and that they have, as much as is possible, a genuine contact with the local inhabitants. The bed and breakfast plans in country homes seem very satisfactory to us because they allow a relation with the local people. We contest in any case the heavy support

systems; we would like extremely light tourism structures. Campgrounds, for example, are not totally de-
structive: when the campers leave, nature reappears.

And we are totally uncompromising on the question
of highways, because no element destroys the natural
environment more. If people want to know nature,
they should work a little at it. In the same way, we are
opposed to motorboats and favorable to sailboats, and
opposed to ski lifts—if people want to ski, let them
learn to climb, to hike a little, it will do them a lot of
good. And if people want to know the forest, let them
cross it on foot rather than in their cars. This is a very
important point.

The first time I criticized highways before a tribunal
of experts from M.I.A.C.A., one of them said to me:
"So you are a partisan of an aristocratic tourism and
against a democratic tourism." That is very revealing.
Walking is aristocratic; cruising in your car is democratic. And, I might add, it is not entirely false, because you have to love nature already to enjoy walking
in it. This presupposes a kind of refinement that is
foreign to the vacationers who speed down the highway
as they are later going to speed on the Bassin d'Arcachon
in their launches. They see nothing, understand nothing, learn nothing of this different world; they know
only one thing: how to get a tan. Thus we have this
viewpoint: nature is not only a place where one goes for
a vacation, it is a world to discover, to penetrate, in
company with its inhabitants.

*You want this region of Aquitaine to become a sort of
model for a new tourism?*

If we could, yes. And a kind of awakening is taking place. More and more people are realizing that it is not possible to crisscross the forest with highways or build huge tourist complexes on the beaches. City governments are beginning to realize the consequences of such projects. And we see people, even very uncultivated people, developing an astonishing degree of political consciousness. Some oldtimers of our region one day brought us documents dating from the fifteenth century guaranteeing usufructuary rights to the forest of La Teste. And one of them was able to expound on the subject better than a lawyer.

Didn't you have the feeling that you were defending a lost cause?

We never lost hope of winning. But we knew well that we were unequally matched in our fight. M.I.A.C.A. had behind it money, the support of politicians, the continuity of succeeding governments, and the simple fact that it is composed of personnel that give all their time to it, whereas we were acting as volunteers in addition to our work. And the times we succeeded in blocking a project, we saw it reappear in the same form three or four years later. Of course, a large number of these maniacal projects were abandoned. But M.I.A.C.A. won on certain idiotic projects (the gulf of Lacanau) simply by perseverance. The vices of M.I.A.C.A. were sometimes officially recognized (the revenue court made a much talked-of report against it) and the economic crisis has somewhat slowed its activities.

What was your particular involvement in this affair?

You might say I was at first an assistant to Bernard Charbonneau; then when he became tired, he went into retirement, and I became president of the defense committee. And when I in turn had too much work, a team of younger people took over.

But I'd like to come back to the reason why I gave so much time to this fight. I committed myself totally because M.I.A.C.A. embodies in an overt and monstrous way three elements I detest: technocracy, the bureaucratic attitude, and capitalist power.

It is a technocracy totally indifferent to the human environment as well as to the natural environment, saying, "There should be ten thousand tourists here," and marking a red dot on a map at a place where it is simply not possible to put them if one knows the area. And there is a bureaucratic attitude that makes it impossible to obtain information. The mission periodically publishes magnificent books on its work. You read them, you do a detailed criticism of them, and they reply: "But these documents are completely outdated." You respond, "Then show us the definitive plans." "That is impossible. It's like life, they never cease to change." Every time you criticize a project, they put forward another one that was published later. This is a very revealing example of administrative secrecy, which is really our bête noire, the enemy we face continually. How can you hope to develop self-management, how can people have some kind of power over their futures, as long as they are given incomprehensible plans that include tricks the layman cannot detect? I recall the map for the expropriation of land on Cape Ferret. I knew the plan included an expressway paralleling the present highway and going straight through the forest. It didn't appear on the map. I went to inquire in the proper departments, and after some hesitation, they told me, "Yes, that's true." And they showed me on the map a line finer than a hair, almost invisible, representing the expressway. On the scale of the map, it should have been at least two millimeters wide. This is the kind of trickery, representative of one kind of administrative bureaucrat, that we constantly encountered with M.I.A.C.A.

You and other committee members own villas on the Aquitaine coast. Don't people say to you: "You are aristocrats defending your territory against invasion by vacationing workers"?

The majority of committee members are not property owners. And—this is my own personal idea—I would be very favorable to the elimination of the privileges of this private property. I would accept quite readily that villa owners would occupy them something like one month during the summer and the rest of the time would be obliged to put them at the disposition of an administration allowing others to use them. This is similar to the rotation instituted by Russia in some of the most beautiful parts of the Black Sea coast. But of course this implies that people don't necessarily take their vacations at the time they wish.

So you advocate co-ownership or shared use of property?

Rather, a shared use.

Doesn't this attack the essence of the right to private property?

The plans for land expropriation do so at least as much. I think it is important that through an expanded scheduling we can accommodate five times as many tourists without augmenting the number of beds and the support system that destroys the human and natural environments.

But we had another goal for the Aquitaine region: to maintain and develop the local trades instead of eliminating them. And I'm not only thinking of oyster farming. There is a lumber industry in the Landes forest, and I would like to know why most houses built by M.I.A.C.A. are of cement and not, as in Canada, of local wood. Even for large buildings, the Canadians use large-size prefabricated panels of pine. This practice contributes to the actual development of local work. Asking for it here shows that our main interest is in local populations, tourists taking only second place. It is necessary that the inhabitants be protected first: this nature is their place of residence, their means of a real occupation. Local activities must be developed to the advantage of craftsmen, small businessmen, and farmers; neither the tourist's interests nor the so-called general interests of the economy should be put ahead of them.

But obviously, the tourist is a city dweller, middle-class (or lower middle-class), and a motorist, three main characteristics that make it inevitable that an administration such as M.I.A.C.A. put their wishes first.

11.

Toward a Forum-Style University

MADELEINE GARRIGOU-LAGRANGE: *We have hardly mentioned your profession. You said the other day that you were pushed into law by your father; then you chose a university career—more precisely, that of professor of Roman law—because of your love for history and teaching, but also with a sort of ironic pleasure at becoming an unnecessary parasite on society.*

JACQUES ELLUL: That is quite right.

It was a very aristocratic view of life.

Aristocratic or anarchist?

Both of them, wasn't it?

Maybe my position was at heart aristocratic, I don't know. It was explicitly anarchist: "I profit from them and exploit them."

You are interested in so many things; were you uninterested in your profession?

At the very beginning, I couldn't see myself in a professor's robe, speaking to a hundred and fifty students. And then, fairly soon, I came to love it, less for what I taught than for the students. I have to admit that I was caught in the trap of my original irony; I didn't teach Roman law in such a way that it was devoid of meaning or interest. It wasn't a profession for me. Faced with a group of students, I tried to transmit something to them, to respond, you might say, to searching minds. When I sensed their searching, I tried to find something in my teaching—even in Roman law—that could respond to them. And since it has always annoyed me abominably to say the same thing twice, I changed my courses every year, accumulating a variety of things. I wanted to do something that interests me while interesting the students.

Have you always taught Roman law?

I did for years. At the beginning, I was the Romanist who juggled with Roman law, only analyzing the text. And progressively, by reintegrating law into its context of society, in restoring to it its historical dimension, I

was led to become less and less a Romanist and more
and more a historian.

*Your profession is the area of least commitment, of least
personal involvement in your life, isn't it?*

I wouldn't quite say that; for example, you can't discount that in 1946, at the time when the Institute of
Political Studies at Bordeaux was being set up, I asked
that Marxist thought be offered as a course. If I'm not
mistaken, it was the first such course in France, and I
taught it for more than thirty years.

That is a long way from Roman law.

Basically, there was still my profession of historian of
institutions. I was familiar with the methods of the pure
historian, the study of archives. Moreover, I couldn't
dissociate all this from the study of law and society.
And since I tried to be honest in my courses—not
perfectly honest, but as honest as possible—I made
every effort to keep myself from transmitting either my
Christian beliefs or my Marxist tendencies while teaching. But at the same time, I tried to make my teaching
conform to my personal thinking.

So I taught both a course on Marx and one on the
sociology of Technique at the Institute of Political
Studies. And I should mention that teaching contrib-
uted a lot to me: first, through the relations with the
students. They gave me no rest; I could never slack off,
because I was constantly faced with young people who

demanded something serious, new, and ever more thorough. I was forced to progress to be able to teach something that had meaning, or perhaps that gave meaning.

Only something intellectual, or were they looking for a mentor?

I have never claimed to be in any way a mentor. I have never tried to convert or indoctrinate anyone. I have never taught my thought or put forth my beliefs as truth. On the contrary, out of honesty, when I had something to say, for example, on Christianity, I warned the students that as a Christian I could involuntarily modify things and that they should maintain a critical attitude. In the same way, in my courses on Marx, I warned them that my goal was not to make them Marxists or anti-Marxists but to give them intellectual tools to help them make an informed choice. If I was at times a mentor for some, it was always involuntarily. But in the intellectual domain, I was stimulated. I realized that if I didn't read the books they read, if I didn't see the films they saw, I would turn off the students. To be able to tell them things, even in Roman law, that would open them up to the world and to life, I had to fit into their cultural universe. Therefore they stimulated me to work. When they became interested in Foucault, I read Foucault because they read him and not because he particularly interested me.

For your teaching, or for individual relations you had with one student or another?

Always for my teaching. But teaching implied numerous individual relations. My students, and even others
who had heard of me, have always somewhat swamped
me in coming to me with their complicated problems.

After saying this, I realize today that I have rarely
worked entirely out of selfless motives, for the simple
reason that I liked what I did. I almost always have
worked with a group in mind, to furnish the answer
people wanted.

*In the beginning of your career, you undoubtedly had much
smaller classes than today, and the students were more
socially homogeneous. The influx of students into the university has probably greatly changed many factors in the
prospect of university education in the future.*

Due to my age, I have had very little experience of the
very large classes. Two hundred and fifty students was
the largest class I had, and that is still a lot. As I have
taught only doctoral courses at the school of law for the
last fifteen years or more, I have very small classes,
allowing me to do personal teaching. I know each one
of my students; I know what each one can do. So I
haven't experienced this particular change, but another: the incredible difficulty of relations with colleagues. We don't see each other any more. This is due
to the campus design, to the dispersion of courses, and
to the professors' overload—they go from committee
meetings to board meetings. It's incredibly and ab-
surdly complicated. And it is part of the overall mal-
function of the university, which I believe no longer
fulfills at all its initial purpose.

Have you ever tried to play an active role in the university, as a dean, for example?

I could have been one, of course. But I didn't want to, after a brief experience that I didn't want to pursue.

Because you preferred other commitments?

Certainly, but also—this will seem very pretentious— because at the time the role of dean was very paternalistic and not very effective, and because I had no interest in taking care of the administrative management of the school. Administration really does not interest me.

Have you ever considered the possibility that it is the price we have to pay for an autonomous university?

In 1968 I really had a great deal of hope that the universities would become truly autonomous and would once again take full initiative in their teaching and their exams. I believed that university reforms could serve as a platform for an ideological transformation. And I still have this goal. I always come back to a revolutionary goal: that the universities no longer turn out good little technicians who will make capable executives but nonentities; on the contrary, I would like to see them impart knowledge to men and also train them to do a fundamental criticism of this knowledge and of the world they live in (and of their lives). Then the justificatory ideologies and powers of any kind will be constantly questioned, not in order to destroy them but to allow each person to exercise freedom. In this way, and I would say in this way alone, a permanent process of revolution would be set in motion. I believe that social transformation can only begin with transformation of business executives, hence the importance of transforming the education of these executives. This is what I hoped would result from 1968.

What kind of transformation are you talking about?

When we developed the idea of a critical university (a term that was borrowed by the Marxists and has come to mean a Marxist university—a Marxist university would not be any more critical, but just as dogmatic as the present one), we were thinking of a university that would not only dispense knowledge but also open students to a critical attitude toward this knowledge. There is in the university a strict dichotomy between these two things. Classical professors limit themselves to dispensing knowledge, whereas certain groups— Marxists, for example—do nothing but critical analyses, which is a mistake. Modern pedagogues claim that knowledge has no value in itself, that memorization is worthless. Even in the elementary grades, they claim that they awaken the mind without using the disciplines for the acquisition of knowledge. How absurd: you don't become a painter by applying colors at random but by assiduously learning to draw. For Picasso to achieve his final stage, he had to be the excellent draftsman he was at the beginning. There is no inspiration or intelligence without discipline. The mind is not developed in the abstract but by beginning with a certain number of facts. One must acquire knowledge and memorize it to be able to think, to innovate, to reason, and to progress.

Were you favorable to 1968?

I agreed with most of the early student demands. I had been well acquainted with the situationists for many years, and they saw quite thoroughly what kind of revolution was necessary. They inspired the style, the form, and the wording of the slogans for the revolutionary thrust. When the students demanded a transformation of the culture, an upheaval of teaching and university structures, and autonomy for the universities—

But what do you mean by that?

Obviously that the university, each university, rule itself, choose its professors, its programs, and its type of exams; that there be no more national department of education, or worse, a department of universities; that the university be independent of the political powers; that it make its own rules and laws; that it no longer depend in any way on the government. That is the essential requirement for a change of society. It presupposes a political power that is generous . . . furnishing the money and leaving the university free. That was the dream. As long as the students asked for this, they were right, and they came close to succeeding. It was all lost when they tried to make the revolution—to overthrow de Gaulle and put the working class in power. As if a real revolution can be made with barricades in the streets in the style of 1848, or even 1917! The students confused a feasible localized revolution with the myth of revolution itself. At that point I was opposed to their movement, because it was obviously heading for failure. And the slogans like "more burning summers" or "it is only the beginning" exasperated me with their lack of realism; they were singing the same old songs, while trying to hide their failure. It was one more error caused by the Marxist interpretation of events, or actually, by the application of a code derived from Marxism (class struggle, revolution possible through the working class alone, etc.).

Do you believe that a new revolution in the university is possible?

I prefer calling a spade a spade. There is no more university. The concept of a global education that develops the mind, the thinking, and the personality and instigates true research no longer exists. We manufacture little technicians, that's all, each one useful in his slot.

But I will also say that, having a clean slate, we must make something else, recreate a true university, a truly interdisciplinary *universitas* where independent people can teach independently. I believe that this orientation, in my opinion essential, is historical. In other words, I give the French university less than ten years to go to the dogs. Then something else will have to be created and I am sorry I will be too old to take part in it.

You say this movement is historical. Do you see the first fruits of it yet?

No. We did see some small efforts by students who started a few projects, saying, for example: "We will choose for ourselves our subjects for study and we will call on such-and-such a professor, not to teach us but to be a partner and to discuss with us the subjects of our choosing."

Isn't this a revival of the university of the Middle Ages?

Of course. It corresponds pretty closely to one version of the university of the Middle Ages.

But isn't it incompatible with a university for the masses?

The model I have often dreamed of seems to me to be historically accurate yet inconceivable in our day: it consists of a multiplicity of technical schools preparing for the occupations, and in addition, a completely gratuitous university, that is, one that serves no purpose.

A forum-style university?

Something like that, where entry is not dependent on exams but on areas of interest.

You brought up the question of the masses. But it is not the right question. Who are the masses? Why do they want to enter the university? Why must the university actually be accessible to all no matter what their social origins? The modern argument responds that it is because access to the university has the appearance of being a privilege and because a diploma is the key to certain careers. But imagine the radical separation I would like to see: the technical school and the *universitas*. On the one side, anyone with competence can enter; on the other side, no entrance requirements, but the masses will not beat down its doors because it will have no practical advantage. It would be very elitist, but it would be an elite composed of students of the working class as well as upper middle-class or country origins. This elite will not necessarily come to power, but will surely criticize those in power.

No diplomas in this university.

The diploma has only a utilitarian purpose. That they be given in technical schools and institutes that train electrical engineers, chemists, judges, or doctors, I agree with completely. But I observe in all domains the need for something else. For example, now when history is disappearing from the teaching curriculum, people are fascinated by history. Students ask for it, unlike the situation twenty-five years ago. Workers, too, have asked my permission to attend one or another of my classes, social history, for example. There's no need to have a diploma to attend classes, and I assure you they were more motivated to study my sections on labor unions than many of my students.

This in my opinion resolves the question of an open or closed university. If you want a university that dispenses useful professional diplomas, it should be closed and selective. It is quite necessary that medical students learn to perform an operation and that an engineer's bridges don't collapse with the first truck that passes over. Selectivity is justified in these domains.

But there is no reason to institute a selection either at the entry or at the departure from the university that gives a critical education based on human experience and stimulates a search for meaning in those individuals who think that they exist only if they spend their lives searching for true meaning.

We are far afield from the present university.

They have absolutely nothing in common, but I feel it will come about because a profound, latent demand does exist.

I have, by the way, experienced in a small way this perfectly gratuitous characteristic of education at the very beginning of the Institute of Political Studies, and I was never so happy. It served no purpose; a few students came there and they were passionately interested in the questions we treated. That's all there was to it. It was obviously the ideal class. They were not looking for a diploma but for an education in politics that was not available anywhere else, on Marx, on the structure of the political parties. It was a marketplace for ideas.

Yet it was characterized by the fact that only young people, students moreover, who had not yet entered professional life, came there.

Of course. But I think that a university of this kind, provided it is accessible through scholarships to people who don't have sufficient means, should be open to all who want this kind of intellectual and critical training, regardless of age, background, or educational qualifications.

And in your opinion, teachers for this kind of university could be found?

I can find you a whole batch of them immediately.

From among the present professors?

Of course. Some of my colleagues give free seminars in addition to their official teaching, simply because students are interested in a subject.

And to continue with this utopia, do you think such a university would accommodate full-time professional teachers?

I believe that either the professors will accept a more modest lifestyle in view of the importance of this work of intellectually and culturally transforming the world, or else we could find professors to divide their time between paid teaching and the *universitas.*

You mentioned a utopia. Assuredly it is utopian to put together from scratch a model such as this one. But I am telling you that this will happen in the next ten years. The state will never allow such a valuable machinery as the university to escape from its clutches. The present political power in France will never tolerate the development of disciplines that have no use and produce nothing—history, sociology, and philosophy —but serve only to furnish critical references. It is not insignificant that the present minister of education has for the past five years systematically destroyed the university body. And if it is rebuilt on the fringes and it obtains the results I hope for, it will be the site of a political battle. It will be the same no matter who is in power, the liberal socialists or the communists, the liberal gaullists or the fascists.

12.

Theology and Technique

MADELEINE GARRIGOU-LAGRANGE: *It is time, I think, to bring up a particularly important subject in your life: the work you have labored at for something like forty years. How did this project take shape with you?*

JACQUES ELLUL: I have already told you how I felt I had two loyalties: one to a socio-Marxist interpretation and one to the biblical revelation. The starting point of my work was, first, the desire to express what I believed as a Christian; and since I was an intellectual, my work was that of an intellectual intent on being conscious of his Christian faith. Moreover, I could not disregard the concrete positions I had taken in regard to society or abandon the hope I had of a revolution. In other words,

Christianity for me could only be lived and conceived in relation to this society, to this moment in history, to the goal of changing the world.

From the outset there was, then, this sort of duality in my thought and my research. But despite that, I can't say that by 1937 or 1939 I already had the idea of constructing a series of works based on these two elements. At the time, I wrote articles with one emphasis or the other. Yet I recall that the first fairly long article I wrote in 1938 was a commentary (surely very simplistic and elementary) on the prophet Micah as prophet of the revolution; the article has been misplaced somewhere, but it is very representative. And then I became certain that I could not rest indefinitely in two domains and two differing modes of thought without establishing a link between them. This relation was evident for certain elements of Marxism that could not be understood outside of Christianity.

But then I had to face a temptation: that of monism. Here was my approximate intellectual path from 1940 to 1955: could I bring all of history, all of human invention into a Christian perspective? In other words, was synthesis possible? As a historian, and more specifically, as a Romanist, I didn't think it was possible to make a synthesis of Latin thought, Roman law, and the Roman form of government, with the biblical revelation on man and society. The two seemed as perfectly antinomical to me as Greek philosophical thought to Hebrew and New Testament thought. Neither synthesis nor accord was possible.

Should we then give in to this other fault frequent in

Christianity: since synthesis is impossible, since antithesis is obvious, shall we exclude, condemn, damn? Based on the Christian point of view, shall we say that the Romans did not really practice law because they did not know Jesus Christ? Shall we judge, as we have done since the sixteenth century when we began to invade the world, that pagan societies are not really societies, since Christianity alone permits a good political system, acceptable laws, and a satisfactory economic organization? I reacted as a historian to such judgments: this exclusion is intolerable. Roman society aroused my admiration too much for me to say that what the Romans accomplished has no value or importance. So I also had to accept that laws, morals, and political systems have their value outside of Christianity.

I was sidetracked for too long by this problem. I did develop in 1942–43 a plan of work in two columns, but I still had a hard time seeing, as I laid it out, the relation between the two. It remained, if I may use the word, pretty schizophrenic.

At that time I planned, on the theological side, a series of exegetical and theological Bible studies, and on the other side, given the great deficiency of Protestantism in this area, a search for ethics from a political perspective, in which I would find how the Christian life can be expressed collectively, under the conditions of *this* society (which must consequently be understood). That was the task.

Protestantism has developed a theology I consider quite remarkable, but this theology has never been able to yield concrete results; there has always been, as I have said many times, a gap between theology and life.

Moreover, Protestants have a peculiarity that is seldom remarked: as soon as a great theologian contributes something, Protestants discount it in less than one generation, and look for something else. There is no continuity of thought! This is what happened to the greatest theologian of our time, Karl Barth. In the domain of ethics, no one has succeeded in beginning with his thought and arriving at a result. Insofar as my training was oriented toward the concrete and not toward philosophy, I thought that the search for ethics should have primacy in my works.

I thus planned out two lines of study. From the theological standpoint, there was a biblical exegesis that would be primarily an exegesis of the Old Testament. After Luther's and Barth's commentaries on the Epistle to the Romans, it was not worth the trouble to do another one, and at that time I thought the Gospels were clear and easily understood. So I was especially attracted by the Old Testament. It seemed astonishingly rich, with many facets and meanings. That is why I wrote biblical commentaries on the books of Kings, Jonah, and Job (the latter has never been published). I also searched the Old Testament for the foundations of an ethic, and this led me progressively to construct one. First was an introduction to ethics entitled *To Will and to Do*, then *The Ethics of Freedom*, and now *The Ethics of Holiness*, which I am in the process of preparing, then—

Along the other line, I planned primarily a study of technical society. For I asked myself this question. "If Marx lived in 1940, what would he consider the fundamental element of society, what would he choose as the basis for his study? In the nineteenth century, when economics was the deciding factor, the development of capitalism was this most significant element. Today it is no longer economics but Technique. Capitalism is a historical fact that is already obsolete. It may well last another century, but it has no more historical importance. What is new, significant and determinant (Marx always maintained that we must study the factor that is determinant at a given moment) is the development of Technique.

Therefore I was certain, absolutely certain, that if Marx were alive in 1940 he would no longer study economics or the capitalist structures, he would study Technique. So I began to study Technique, using a method as similar as possible to the one Marx used a century earlier to study capitalism.

All of the work I conceived during that period was intended to be, with few exceptions, part of the detailed analysis of this technical society. For example, *The Technological Society* studies this society in its entirety; *Propaganda* examines the technical methods that are used to change opinion and transform the individual; *The Political Illusion* is the study of what politics becomes in a technical society; *The Metamorphosis of the Middle-Class Man*[1] looks at the social classes in a technical society. My two books on the revolution [*Autopsy of Revolution* and *From the Revolution to Revolts*] pose the question of what kind of revolution is possible in a technical society. *The Technological System*

---

1. *Metamorphosis, From the Revolution to Revolts,* and *The Mindless Tyranny* are not available in English. —TRANS.

raises another problem: Technique as a system within technical society, or in other words, what new insights can we gain from the application of systems analysis to the technical phenomenon? And finally, *The Mindless Tyranny* is the study of what art becomes in the technical environment. These are some examples of my work, as I posed each question in the technical society.[2]

You thus took off in two completely different fields at the same time. Did you try, in order to help them meet, to bring theology to the aid of sociology?

I inevitably had to ask myself the question of their relationship. I felt very early—I remember having done a long report on the subject in 1947 for the Ecumenical Council—that a relation of mutual criticism should exist between the two. Sociology should be the means of criticizing theology, and vice versa. In other words, theology always seemed to me as though it were tempted to drift off into the heavens, ignoring the real situation of living human beings that it ought to be addressing. Sociology, then, should be the instrument that helps

---

2. I insist on the use of the word "Technique," the only correct word, whereas the trend or habit is going to the use of "technology," in imitation of the American vocabulary. It is a totally incorrect usage. Technology is a discourse on Technique (it can be either the teaching *of* a given technique, or a philosophy or sociology of Technique), but it is not Technique itself! An automobile mechanic who repairs a carburetor does not use technology. But politicians and intellectuals speak importantly of the development of technology in speaking of Technique. [The etymological meanings of *technique* and *technology* are the same in English as in French. —Trans.]

me determine, within theology, what is useful, shall we say. It provides the possibility of communicating today a living word, of discovering a new lifestyle for humanity by eliminating the elements of subtlety and purely intellectual demonstration.

One could write tons of books on questions that are not real questions. Even though he, too, often expounded gratuitous theology, Barth proved to be an extremely useful teacher in this respect. I will cite for you just one of his jokes over a subtle question posed by a student: "Do you really believe that the serpent spoke as Genesis describes?" "The question is not at all important," Barth replied. "We need not know whether or not the serpent spoke, but it is important to know what he said." There are countless intellectually stimulating questions like this, false questions leading to fixed thinking and having nothing to do with theology. The fundamental and pertinent questions all deal with the human being. The human being is not interested in knowing whether the serpent talked but that the serpent proposed to man to become like God. Take, for example, the problem of the Virgin Mary. It was obviously important in an era when Christians had to define themselves in relation to mystery religions that also had virgin mothers. Or later, it was important in the fourteenth to sixteenth centuries because of the debate on tradition and the Scriptures, first, and second, on the method of interpreting Scripture (nominalism, realism, symbolism, etc.). But in itself it is certainly not an important problem for all times and all societies. Sociology seemed to me a very useful instrument in sorting out within theology that which is timely from that which is not.

So you tried to identify, with the aid of sociology, the theological questions that are important for man today?

Exactly. And I used sociology as an instrument of criticism. I really could not accept that there are highly specialized intellectual methods to apply to every kind of object. For me, a theological method should include a sort of philosophical confrontation, a sociological method, an instrument for the observation of facts, and so on. It is possible that my training as a historian had something to do with it, because the historians play several parts; they can't avoid being part sociologist, part theologian, part philosopher.

The sociological method itself seemed to me, then, to be a critical method applicable to the work of theologians. But inversely, I could not accept a sociology that is limited to understanding the purely objective mechanisms of human societies while excluding the question of their meaning. With the introduction of mathematical methods, sociology claims to be more and more scientific, but what value is there in a sociological work that excludes the meaning of how people live in a given group?

When they want to be purists, sociologists begin by stating that they will not deal with that area. Gurvitch, for example, in studying the phenomena of law, declares: "Yes, of course there is a problem of values in law, but values are the domain of metaphysicians. I examine law only as a sociological phenomenon without concerning myself with values." To an argument of this kind, I offer this theological response: "Insofar as law is a human phenomenon and human beings do not live without giving a meaning to their lives, you cannot study law without studying values." Fortunately, people are coming back to this new perspective, even in the scientific field, discovering the major role of myth in every human group.

Aren't there two ways of proceeding: one consisting of ob-serving the values of the groups you are studying, values that are objective for you and subjective for them; the other consisting of taking into account only the meaning attributed by the one who observes and analyzes?

Assuredly; but first, I would prefer not to talk about the subjective nature of values: for the person who believes in them, they are objective. And besides, I condemn myself to comprehend nothing if I don't enter into the perspective and belief of the person who trusts in these values. Haven't we heard enough of these pseudo-scientific rationalistic discourses, on the church, for example, that show only that those who are speaking understand nothing of their subject? In other words, in my opinion you cannot practice any human science without empathizing with the human being you are study-ing: this empathy is one of the guarantees of objectivity.

Don't you think that your analysis is based on your theologi-cal conception of man's destiny, of the calling God has given him?

I asked myself that question very early on. I don't believe I used theological criticism in that way. I didn't judge the whole on the basis of the values I could identify in the culture as Christian. And that is why, besides, I distinctly dissociated the two lines of study.

To come back to the contribution of theological criticism to sociology, I believe it consists in its requiring us to consider the human phenomenon in its totality instead of separating it into parts. But we must not believe that because a method claims to be rational and scientific, it really is. All you need to do is observe the vast majority of methods today.

We discover, in addition, that to appear scientific, a method often starts out by delimiting its object by eliminating some embarrassing factors: for example, "For simplification, values are defined as ideology and do not concern us." Another example: "Man has always been mistaken to believe in justice." Once these factors are pushed aside, the human phenomenon, the group phenomenon, or the society phenomenon are studied through the use of a supposedly scientific tool that in reality is not at all scientific, because it began by amputating the object. This has been condemned for several years under the name of reductionism. The first example was the famous *homo oeconomicus* of the beginning of the nineteenth century. Human beings were reduced to their economic activity; they were postulated on the basis of their relation to the growth of wealth, and this model was used as though it really depicted human beings. One reason for Marx's greatness was precisely this, that he wanted to reintegrate the totality of the human being in a scientific study of economy and society.

You would say, then, that reductionism consists of amputating the most human aspects of man from man the object?

As I see it, yes, but this is a value judgment. I really am forced to recognize that for the past three thousand years, Mediterranean peoples have believed in the value of justice. I cannot say it is an illusion, or they are mistaken, or it is stupidity. It is scientifically false to study humanity while leaving aside this value of justice. Thus theology forces me to make a critical judgment of any method in sociology or political science.

Why does theology force you to do so?

Because it reveals to me that people are whole, human, and indivisible, that they were created, that they remain in relationship with a transcendent being. I grant you, it is a bias, my personal bias. I don't say that philosophy could not say the same thing, but theology gives me a transcending revelation, teaching me that the first man is created ambivalent, ambiguous, and contradictory in himself. He is created earth, Adam, red earth, clay, and he receives within himself not a soul but the breath of God. He is created to be the image of God (*him* and not a fraction or a part of him, not just his reason or his sense of justice, etc.); and at the same time he is on the order of the animals (God causes all the animals to pass before him to see if he will find an animal similar to himself). He is created having a true relation with God, and at the same time he is free to break away. And in the separation, God maintains a relation. Thus men and women are not simple beings but ambivalent ones.

So when someone comes to me saying, "I study the

clay," I answer, "No, that won't work." And it doesn't work any better when the theologian claims to study the spirit of God in mankind. You must take into account the duality of human nature, this constant confrontation within (which is not just the simple conflict of good and evil). It is demonstrated by the preacher of Ecclesiastes when he said both, "All is vanity," and, "You have put into us the desire for eternal life." This is the key element that allows us to carry out a mutual criticism of sociology and theology.

Your work thus took off on two almost parallel paths. Did these paths have a tendency to meet as your work progressed?

No. It would be more accurate to say that a system of relations appeared between them. By the way, I was amused to realize after the fact that some of my books corresponded to certain others I had written, without my ever having planned it that way. I recently received a letter in which someone told me: "I just read your *Technological System*, and I suddenly saw that your book on hope, *Hope in Time of Abandonment*, had answered it in advance." This was not the result of any plan, but it's very true. On the other hand, I really had planned that *The Ethics of Freedom* would be the dialectical counterpoint to my studies on Technique.

We have not yet said much about freedom. And yet it is at the center of my whole life and my whole work. Nothing I have done, experienced, or thought makes sense if it is not considered in the light of freedom. This is so, first, because the God revealed in the Bible is above all the liberator. He creates for freedom. And when men break their relation with him, God respects this act of independence. The only problem is not the metaphysical question of freedom but how to be assured that we are liberated by God in Jesus Christ, and how to live this freedom. Hence an ethic of freedom.

And are you still working on both fronts at the same time?

Yes, I always carry on simultaneously a theological or biblical study and a sociological study.

Without detriment to other works that fall within the province of your profession of legal historian. Could we say these works are outside of the dual path?

Not entirely. I did conceive of my thesis and the four volumes of legal history as a professional work. My colleagues did not receive them as such. When my *History of Institutions* was published between 1954 and 1958, it provoked rejection and heated criticism from several historians. They charged that it was completely off the track in that it was endowed with an interpretation.

I had, however, tried to do the work of an honest historian, to sum up what I had taught and studied in the historical field for fifteen years. But it is true that I felt that one could not study law in itself, that it was one human phenomenon among others and that one could not explain it without studying at the same time the economic context, the ideological context, the dominant values, and the political connections of the time.

I thus wrote a history of institutions in which law was indeed the main element but was tied to a lot of other things. For I don't think it is possible to study any legal institution if you leave out the system of beliefs from which it arose.

Did you write the history of society as seen through its laws?

Exactly, and this departed greatly from what was usually done. I was also criticized because it wasn't sufficiently "scientific" (in the reductionist sense) and there was a meaning to it. Honestly, I hadn't tried to find one.

You were criticized for having a specific interpretation of society?

I maintain that all history is a specific interpretation of society. My colleagues who wrote a pointillist history, studying a particular element, and who claimed to do a purely objective history, were nonetheless part of an ideological system that made them regard history through a certain framework. That was the common historical method in 1930, and it is even the one I used in my thesis on the *mancipium*, a study in historical criticism that was totally conformist and purely exegetical. Yet I did begin the book with this quotation from Saint Augustine, revealing my interests in 1936 but having nothing to do with the *mancipium*:

> Such is the error of those who cannot accept that what was permitted to the just of ancient times is not permitted to the just of today and cannot accept that God has given a commandment to one and another commandment to another for

temporal reasons. What is permissible now will cease to be so in an hour; what is permitted or commanded there is expressly prohibited and punished here. Does this mean that justice is varied and changeable? No, but the times it governs change as they pass, because they are times.

This shows that I already had a conception of the relativity of institutions and the relativity of their validity. The *mancipium*, an institution that, to summarize roughly, allowed a father to sell his son, was perhaps very valid, after all, in the Roman society of that era. At any rate, it is not something we can judge with our values, but rather it forces us to place ourselves in the system of ideological and mythical values of those whose institutions we study.

To sum it up, even at the time when I did a purely historical and Romanist critical exegesis, I had this preoccupation—what meaning can this institution have? This preoccupation reappears twenty years later in my history of institutions.

Let's leave this side issue to come back to your global project. You said you conceived and formulated it in the forties and fifties. Do you still have the same plan now?

Yes, but it changes. For example, it is obvious that I no longer analyze the Christian ethic in the same terms I used between 1945 and 1950. But the project itself remains: an *ethic* stemming from a biblical theology. For me to finish this project that I developed in precise detail in the early fifties would take a miracle of longevity. My project is too vast—it would comprise eight volumes, and I have only written four so far.

How do you work? Do you have a method?

I always have several books under way, several subjects for books that I try to correlate to each other by maintaining a reciprocal questioning and a dialectical process. My work method is approximately as follows: from the moment I begin working on a subject, I stop reading anything whatsoever that relates to it. I thus work in the opposite order of usual academic method. I think and gather notes sometimes for years; in this way I have files on eight or ten different subjects. When I feel I have enough notes, references, and personal analyses on the question, when my thinking seems to have matured, I write a first draft. Then I begin to read everything there is on the subject; and based on what I have read, I rework my first draft, I modify it, I eliminate views I realize are unsupportable, I rework the plan, and I arrive at a final draft. That is my method, in which the documentary element comes after the thought element.

After and before?

Only after. I try to take every question from scratch.

And all the files you have gathered?

They are files of ideas, my personal notes.

But they are inspired by your reading over the years.

Undoubtedly, but then it is a case of old cultural reserves that I accumulate and that naturally re-

surface, without reference to any particular author
who has treated the same subject.

Do you also use this method for your books on the Bible?

Absolutely. I take a biblical passage and do the exegesis, which is on several levels. First, and I think it is
an essential attitude, one must read the passage naively,
on a primary level: "It seems to be saying this." Then
when this meaning is obtained, one must apply various
methods of interpretation, such as symbolic, historico-
critical, Christocentric, structural. (Only one seems
inadequate to me—the so-called materialistic interpretation. It contributes nothing.) From this ensemble
of different angles of attack will come levels of comprehension. And lastly, after this detour through the
objective methods, one must reinterpret the text in the
light of what has been learned, but also (since I am a
Christian!) in its spiritual sense, according to the anal-
ogy of faith. And then, when all this process is completed, I refer to ten or twenty important writers who
have already written on the same subject.

*In other words, you don't want to allow your thoughts to be
contaminated by anyone.*

I try, I try! All the while, I know perfectly well that I
am influenced and limited by my cultural setting, by
the confines of my reading, but I would like to write, as
much as possible, in accordance with my own experience. For example, each of my books on Technique is
first a book of my experiences. What I write about

television or films comes from what I have experienced as a television viewer or moviegoer.

We are touching on a trait that I consider important: I never write ideas. I have always attempted to transmit exactly what I have experienced, in objectifying it. I have always thought on the experiential level. And my wife has had a considerable influence in this. I was, before her, pretty much a bookworm; I relied heavily on categories and concepts. She continually brought me back to face the living reality, which is all that counts. From that point on, my thinking was guided by my concrete experience. I tried to think only in relation to what I had experienced and to transmit only what I was capable of living. That is why my work is inevitably incomplete and does not appear to be very systematic. I have never tried to make a theoretical system conceived in itself and for itself.

I claim to be an ordinary man, and I am absolutely convinced of it. I have always seen myself as an ordinary man, immersed in the same environment as everyone else. At the movies, I am an ideal spectator. I laugh when everyone laughs, cry when everyone cries; I am emotional. I am not aloof; I only become aloof later. After returning home, I say to myself: "You reacted in this spot and in this way, and here is how the others reacted." And I carry out a minute notation of all that happened. But I am really a split personality. The one watches a play at the theater, and the other observes the setting. A recollection: I told you that I was trained in painting, but I had no musical education. I had never heard the least bit of music before the age of twenty or twenty-one. One evening, I decided to go to a concert. I felt almost nothing, followed nothing, understood nothing. I was completely bored. But what was passionately interesting to me was the audience, and I spontaneously began to do a psychosociological study of the audience as a whole and of the individuals I could observe. I learned a lot that evening. And music seemed like a strange magic to me.

The exact same thing happened when I went to political meetings or mass marches. I was the typical participant and later the analyst of what had happened.

The proof that I am indeed an ordinary man is that there are always a lot of people who tell me: "What you wrote there is exactly what we felt." The only difference is that I have this ability of verbalizing, of intellectual analysis, that they have developed less than I have. That is the only difference.

And also a desire to systematize.

A very strong desire to systematize and to explain, yes.

Does this confrontation with others that you undertake before the final draft of one of your works take place only with books, with already developed thought, or do you also meet with people who are faced with the same problems, do you form work groups?

It all depends. I work with study groups, groups of students, or Bible study groups, of course, and this corresponds to what we already said about the importance of small groups for political action. And when I am in a group, I always listen to the others; I try to grasp their concerns, hear their questions and objections.

And this has counted greatly in the development of my own thinking. I try to be completely open to receive all that is said, for it informs me of the reality of man today. Then, having heard the questions, I try to find a response. Thus relations and groups have an essential place in my research.

But for the task of research itself, I am a terrible individualist. I am incapable of leading a study group or a workshop (since that is what you're supposed to call them nowadays). I am incapable of a cooperative work. In the past, at conventions where they named committees to draft a report, as a committee member I always worked alone: I wrote *my* text that I submitted to the others. I don't even have a secretary to team up with me. I know this limits considerably my possibilities of work and research. I never have complete bibliographies. I have never read all that I should have read. But (it is obviously reactionary and proud of me) I don't know how to delegate work, and I have no confidence in collaborators. This has, besides, been reinforced by experience. Several times I entrusted research to someone, and it was never done the way I wanted it, except once on the subject of the history of institutions.

They didn't select material the way you do?

There is a totally nonscientific element of intuition. When I read a magazine article, I suddenly see a factor that is to me the important factor. But researchers who read the same article will not see the same thing because they do not have the same intellectual context.

You said you were an ordinary spectator. Apparently you are not the same kind of reader as your researcher.

No doubt, but this takes place on the intellectual level. I am a participant like everyone else in the domain of entertainment, of feeling, of immersion in the crowd, of reactions, of cultural milieu; I don't reject influences.

In other respects, I cannot work with a team because, even from a theological standpoint, I draw not only from my intellectual analysis but also from my personal experience. When I read a biblical passage, I don't first take it apart as a structuralist would. This passage implies to me a challenge of the spiritual experiences I have already had. I will then verify that I have not made any blunders in exegesis or in the theological context in which it was written and received. But all these verifications do not cut off my own spiritual experience from my interpretation of the passage.

Haven't you collaborated with your friend Bernard Charbonneau?

In the intellectual domain, we don't work together, we work in dialogue. Charbonneau says to me: "Your book is worthless for such-and-such a reason. I don't agree at all with what you wrote there," and so on. Very often he causes me to rethink one thing or another.

You have presented yourself as a man of dialogue and collective action: dialogue with your students, with the street gangs; collective action in regard to the coast of Aquitaine, and so on. But your works seem both very personal and very individualized. In spite of all of these readers who rediscover their thinking in yours, don't you have the feeling of being very solitary?

I live in an almost total intellectual solitude and in a fairly great spiritual solitude since the deaths of my closest friends. Only my wife penetrates this solitude and makes it livable. Besides, I have always felt fairly solitary inasmuch as those who ought to listen to what I say never share my concerns. I am also solitary because, as I have already mentioned, I don't try to make disciples, and I refuse to found a school of thought. Whether voluntary or not, such an action always implies a betrayal, or at least a deformation. Also, since I progress continually, every time I have the impression of having sufficiently explained several phenomena, I pass on to something else. Those who become attached to something I wrote at a given moment inevitably find themselves out of touch with my new research.

This intellectual solitude is sometimes hard to bear, but all things considered, it is perhaps neither exceptional nor remarkable. I think that everyone is at the same time alone and wonderfully accompanied and also that, when all is said and done, a serious intellectual always makes his or her way alone.

One thing does surprise me. I think I have never said what I explained just now, that my work forms an ensemble. Now I receive more and more testimonies from people who have realized it. This suggests a lot of patience on their part, since they must have read not one book by chance but fifteen or so. Of course, I can't hope that many people do this.

How do you explain this solitude in regard to the theologians, the leaders of your church, the historians, the sociologists and all who, in a word, work in the same fields as you?

On the spiritual level, I think what is significant is that it is not the theologians but lay people who refer to my writing, saying that it spoke to them. This is precisely my goal: I don't want to enter into theological debates. And professional theologians scorn in general what they consider to be the work of an amateur. As for the leaders of my church, I would say that most of them have not read me. Perhaps this is an ordinary phenomenon, but it is especially strong in Protestantism where everyone knows each other: we see Ellul everywhere, on a committee, on a board. No need to read him, we know very well what he thinks, which isn't necessarily true; they have certain preconceived and contrived ideas about me, and they rely on misinterpretations and attribute to me ideas that are not my own. But after all, "No one is a prophet among his own."

In your opinion, your public image does not correspond to your true self?

Based on some sketchy impressions of me from thirty years ago, people have an image of me as a pessimist, anti-Technique, antireactionary, and so forth. And the Protestant intellectuals have only wanted to remember two booklets on which they based a definitive judgment.

You feel that a caricature of you is going around and not a true picture of you?

Yes. However, most people are disturbed by not being able to know whether to classify me as right-wing or left-wing. A study done around 1950 on the political options of French Protestantism defined me as an independent with this interesting note: "Ellul has anarchist tendencies. He can thus be situated on the right." It is true that at that time, insofar as they were individualists and, as I did, they considered freedom to be a fundamental value, the anarchists were classified as abominable right-wingers. It is funny to see how 1968 changed the perspectives. As for me, I never could classify the anarchists on the right.

Do you consider yourself an anarchist?

The anarchist milieu is the only one in which I often feel perfectly at ease. I am myself there. On the other hand, I am not at ease either in the right-wing milieu, which doesn't interest me, or in the left-wing milieu, for whom I am not overtly a socialist and even less a communist. And I am not at all, really not at all at ease in the milieu of the Christian left. But with anarchists, advocates of nonviolence, conscientious objectors, environmentalists, and also some groups in the socialist labor union, I am very comfortable.

Aren't you nevertheless a partisan of a more rational society?

Oh, no, not at all. On the contrary, I believe that the greatest good that could happen to society today is an increasing disorder. For the factor that is winning is insane disorder—state-controlled order or technical order, it matters little. It is extremely urgent that we conquer zones where man can simply move freely: something like the streets reserved for pedestrians. I am in no way pleading in favor of a different social order. I am pleading for the regression of all the powers of order.

If I understand correctly, you are not a partisan of a universal and definitive anarchism, but you think that disorder working against a more and more restrictive order is the only possible salvation for our present society.

That's correct. And I differ from anarchists in that I do not believe in the possibility of an ideal anarchist society that would function without organization or powers. I say to them: "Let us for the time being keep for human beings the maximum of independence and initiative in all directions. Let us make it possible for them to rediscover in this society, which is taking more and more of it from them, some of their personal potential." As for what will happen in fifty or a hundred years, I put my faith rather in the kingdom of God. At any rate, this current of ideas seems essential to me.

Isn't that precisely what isolates you?

Yes, of course, it isolates me terribly. First, because I don't offer an explanation, a ready-made system. And I refuse to do so quite consciously. Even if I had in my pocket the design for the ideal society and the means to achieve it, I would not give it. I believe, here again, that I am faithful to Marx's thinking: Marx never gave the design for a communist society.

Because the design does not exist.

Believing firmly in the dialectical development of history, Marx was convinced that a stage of history cannot be logically inferred from the preceding one. I think, as he did, that we can only establish the facts of the dialectical process and be sure that from the coming crisis will emerge a new design. Therefore it would be impossible for me to describe this one; and even if I could, I would not, for another reason: I believe above all in the importance of human initiative. As I see it, the most important thing is to restore to man the maximum of his capacities of independence, invention, and imagination. This is what I try to do in stimulating him to think. In my work I try to give him the cards so he can then play his own hand. Not mine. Only the rediscovery of the individual's initiative is radical in these times. And this implies that I do not furnish a program.

At the end of my books, readers are called to take action and make their own decisions, and they surely say to themselves, "This is very annoying. I don't see which action I can take." They would prefer a last chapter in which someone would tell them, "Here is what you must think and do." This last chapter I will never write. Even my ethic does not say to the Christian, "Here is what is good and here is what is evil." It does exactly the opposite. "You are liberated, you are called to be human beings before God. Now decide for yourselves concretely what is to be done."

But don't you say that to bring an end to technical society we must propose very clear and mobilizing action? Isn't this contradictory?

In this kind of work, with my intellectual apparatus I serve as an expert furnishing an analysis that ought to be the best I can make. And I try, through this intellectual analysis, to awaken people to their situation and to their need to intervene. But though I can do this work on the theoretical level, going so far as to provoke an awakening, I cannot dictate praxis. It is indeed correct that my books call for an individual awakening and that they will have no significance unless the awakening results in *collective* kinds of action. But it is not for us to substitute our own ideas for the invention and decision of others. That would have been totally contradictory to our purpose. Although it is true that the principal danger to our society is the disappearance of the individual and of freedom, the fact that we want to call attention to the individual does not mean we substitute ourselves for the individual in actions to be undertaken.

In addition, I encounter another obstacle. Every program founded on our analysis can only be a utopia. Now, I am violently opposed to any utopia because it is the epitome of illusory satisfactions. You have a lovely plan that is utopian, and you remain in one spot, because there is never any concrete action, any tactics that put you on the path to accomplishment. Utopia is the final blow in humanity's death. And it is a very concrete death: the last two great utopias were those visions of idealism and the future known as nazism and Stalinism. Now, motivated by a desire to transform society globally, anyone who makes a panoramic and *final* description of this transformation can only be proposing a utopia.

Based on these two fundamental principles (calling attention to the individual in action, and challenging all utopias), I have two modes of action: on the one hand, I often join the new movements that seem grassroots, in the hope that they will eventually become revolutionary (and up until now it has always failed); on the other hand, we have begun *specific*, local actions outside of the political currents but still attacking the problem of our society at a more decisive depth than is usually done. These actions are to serve as examples, seeking to directly change society in depth (and not through general programs) and to stimulate individuals to do, not the same thing, but actions on the same order.

These actions, however, also had a real influence. They were not symbolic acts. When it is a matter of fighting for a transformation of the church against the administrative powers or for the legitimizing of outcasts, it is very concrete work, just the same as joining with situationists or participating in nonviolent groups. But this kind of action shows the extreme difficulty of taking an idea that radically confronts this society, rendering it concrete, and protecting it from being diverted by some other group.

Finally, I have arrived at this maxim: "Think globally, act locally." This represents the exact opposite of the present spontaneous procedure. Think globally: I have tried to show what this means in *The Technological Society* and *Propaganda*, to refuse analytical, pointillist, specialized thinking. It does no good in understanding modern society to take phenomena case by case, to study, for example, the automobile, or television, or video computers, and so on. For each and every one of these phenomena has its meaning, its power, its effect, only when it is placed in relation to all the others (doctors with teaching, and with bureaucracy, and with computer science, and with the planned economy, etc.). If you separate or isolate a fact, you understand absolutely nothing.

But inversely for action, we have the spontaneous tendency to demand centralized action, through the state, through a decision center that sends down decrees from above; but this can no longer have *any* success. The human facts are too complex and the bureaucracy will become heavier and heavier. From now on, if you really want to act, you must do it beginning from the bottom, on the human scale, locally, and through a series of small actions. Though small in scale, these actions can accommodate all the human potential; this can only be accomplished on a reduced scale. This situation really calls for application of the formula "Small is beautiful."[3]

---

3. English in text. —Trans.

13.

God and the Dialectical Process

MADELEINE GARRIGOU-LAGRANGE: *We have talked about how your thinking was developed. We have talked about your commitments, your profession, and your works. All of this as though it were nothing but fragments, as though you were a fragmented man. And of course you don't see yourself this way. What is the dialectical process that put all this into motion and gives it coherence?*

JACQUES ELLUL: It is true that there is a dialectic within my work, and it is entirely central in that I have discovered progressively that in the world we live in there are no means of thinking and acquiring knowledge that are not of a dialectical nature. But I should point out that this discovery was not a philosophical one, and it did not rely on a prior knowledge of the dialectic. I became conscious, as I worked and thought, that I needed to interpret all things in a dialectical manner.

Marx is one of those who led me to this realization, but I was much more attracted at first by his economic interpretation than by the philosophical aspect of his thought; I will tell you again, I am not a philosopher and I have never been one. Much later I was to realize, again in retrospect, that Christianity and biblical thought are dialectical.

Having said this, I want to clarify that the dialectic presupposes history. It is not enough to pose a positive factor and a negative factor. There has to be a passage of time for the two contradictory factors to come into relationship and be able to give rise to a new situation. As I have already said, Marx does not describe the communist society. He limits himself to saying, "Here are the historical forces whose relationship to each other will be dialectical and will bring about a crisis that will lead into a new phase."

And this phase will include an unknown factor.

Inevitably, for this takes place within history; it does not function as a mechanism would. I thus realized that to grasp the reality of the world we live in, we must take into account the elements that cannot be included in a vast intellectual synthesis. And I completely gave up searching for either a definitive explanation of our time and of history, and for a synthesis that can encompass everything. In other words, I show in my work a systematic mind, but I have refused, you might say systematically, to produce a system.

Since the beginning?

Not entirely, but I have never been tempted by general explanations of history. And it is possible that my Protestant component had a role, confronted as it was with Roman Catholic theology. All the Roman Catholic theologians I read were looking for a synthesis, a complete and satisfying system, whereas in Protestant thought—and I very quickly showed myself to be thoroughly Protestant—contradiction exists. I think that from the beginning of Christianity there has been a sort of passion for unity—bringing everything under a single principle or else carrying out manipulations to obtain a unified system. Every time a contradiction appears, we try to reduce it to the ideal *one,* the unique, the explanation of everything that moves, the reduction to a single dimension, and so on. Now, I believe this is intellectually impossible, spiritually wrong, and concretely dangerous. All the great massacres were done in the name of unity. I am viscerally opposed to all unity. It is also the error of monotheism if the sole God is not himself plural (Jewish Elohim is plural, as is the Christian trinity); this should guarantee a pluralism of thought and an acceptance of contradiction.

Do you mean that Protestant thought is spontaneously dialectical?

Yes. The world is in perpetual contradiction with the will of God; they clash constantly just as God's freedom runs up against man's independence.

Is this the basis for Protestant pessimism?

Yes and no, because everything takes place within grace, and grace is just as unpredictable as a new historical fact in the dialectical process.

At any rate it is a tragic view of the human condition.

I wouldn't call it tragic, because there is no fatalism. It is more a dramatic view. God does not want to rule everything; the world is extraordinarily uncertain, dominated as it is by sin. But within this world are at work grace, the covenant, and the promise. God does not reject his creation, but his relationship with it is one of tension, of conflict, and of pardon.

This is your theological worldview.

It conforms entirely to the Protestant line. But I have recreated it, or at least rethought it, throughout the course of my work. We find ourselves, on the theological level, faced with two elements that can neither be made into a synthesis nor be mutually exclusive. Since the world is what it is, I cannot conclude that God does not exist. Since God is all-powerful, I should not conclude that the world is the result of God's will. There is a contradiction here, and therefore a dialectical process.

But then, looking at the society we live in, I asked myself if and how this society dominated by Technique could evolve according to another logic. The technical system has its own logic, and it is at work within our society, profoundly disrupting it. Can there be an evolution that would not be the absorption of all society, the molding of man and society by Technique? This evolution would require the intervention of a factor that we know cannot be assimilated by Technique.

Technique seemed to me and still seems able to assimilate everything. What can then be the contradicting factor? Could it be the cultures of the Third World? I don't think they measure up, and in saying that I speak not on a metaphysical level but on a historical and sociological level.

Or could I include in this dialectical relation a factor I will call Mankind with a capital M, or human nature? This would presuppose that mankind has enough permanence and autonomy for me to be certain that, no matter what happens, human nature will last. Now, when I look as a historian at past civilizations, I don't see an intangible nature in human beings. I wouldn't go so far as to say that we can understand nothing of the thinking of Egyptians who lived two thousand years before Christ, but I am not sure we can really understand them. And I do not observe any permanence either in the history of societies or in human thought but rather a lot of fluctuations and contradictions. Humans are extraordinarily adaptable and changing beings. I cannot say that there is a definite whole, human nature, on which Technique will break its teeth. Thus it is impossible for me to place a permanent mankind in opposition to Technique as a dialectical factor.

Nature is not permanent, either.

There is no such thing as immutable, intangible nature, whose persistence is guaranteed us (and this is implied if we believe in the creation, though some have concluded the opposite) and whose structure we can consider a law, or laws; it is not a good and true model for us—the great temptation is to say, "We must obey nature." Nature as a group of laws and as a model is of our own making. And as for its concrete reality, we see today how fragile it is. The atom is split, the ocean polluted.

Mankind or nature, neither is sufficient for the foundation of a critical method, nor are they the counterpoint of all-powerful Technique. The latter is an all-encompassing whole that includes mankind and nature. For there to be a chance for change, for a dialectic, there must exist a force completely outside the system. This force that the system is incapable of absorbing can only be God, a transcendent God.

If there is not this transcendent, Technique can absorb everything or destroy everything, lay all to waste, empty mankind of humanity, and annihilate the natural world. This does not mean that, for me, the transcendent is a kind of stopgap. The answer is given to me within the faith, and that is completely different. In other words, I am not brought to accept the God of Jesus Christ because I need a transcendent as a dialectical factor in relation to the assimilating power of Technique. But having accepted the God of Jesus Christ, I affirm that he is our only recourse in the face of Technique.

I do not mean to say that God will intervene directly with Technique, as at the tower of Babel, to cause it to fail. But with the help of God's biblical revelation we can find the lucidity, courage, and hope that will enable us to intervene with Technique. Without these, we can only let ourselves sink into despair. But I must make another clarification on this dialectical relation: God is for me so unlike an answer or an escape that I state the situation in the opposite order. God is the positive, the affirmation, the yes; and in this dialectical process, Technique is the negative, the negation (which, by the way, the Bible indicates). Of course this doesn't mean to say that Technique is evil itself. We have already spoken of the positivity of negativity. It was indeed necessary that human beings become technicians so that history could take place. This reflects the complex relation of the two freedoms.

Do you see only one way out of the human predicament, the theological solution?

The only solution left is through a relationship with God, but not in the simplistic and incantatory manner of B. H. Lévy in regard to the eternal law, transcendent in itself even if God is not. His theory is very embryonic on the subject of the world and the transcendent. I think that humanity can create an escape in referring to the transcendent but not in waiting passively for the transcendent to act. We see in the Bible that God acts through human intermediaries. Human beings must accept to enter into the politics of God. We then have a reversal of the fundamental reality of the dialectical process. In the realm of human history and in our society, Technique actually becomes the positive factor in the dialectical process; the role of mankind bearing the transcendent will necessarily be the negative. But let us remember that the negative is the truly determinant element in the dialectical process, since it forces change.

In aiming a certain number of challenges, objections, and basic criticisms at the foundations, we can make Technique change its orientation and begin, to avoid the word "synthesis," what we might call a new historical period in which it will once again be in its proper place, that of a means subordinated to ends.

You can easily see that I am wrongly called a pessimist. Pessimism is not the word, it is rather a negativity within a dialectical process, and this negativity should permit us to go beyond the earlier stage of positivity, which was static and nonhistorical.

We are in the age of Technique. But for you, whatever the age, God is always the contradicting dialectical factor?

Yes, speaking of God in the history of mankind after the separation. And, on this level and not that of theology, the confrontation of positive and negative is always expressed in a crisis, and the crisis is a period of freedom. What does God do when, acting as the critical factor in human history, he triggers the crisis? He breaks destiny to re-establish a changing situation in which mankind will have an opportunity for freedom.

You see history as a succession of episodes in which, every time, God intervenes?

Not exactly that. There is the history produced by man that tends to unfold as a logical and linear succession, thus without meaning. And there are, not automatically and not every time, but miraculously and unexpectedly, some interventions, advents of God between events, through human beings, changing the course of this history and at the same time permitting human beings to discover a meaning in it or take bearings to find the meaning. This is equivalent to the biblical opposition of *chronos* (time that passes) and *kairos* (the moment of intervention).

So his intervention, through human agency, continually leads us to take new steps.

Yes, but his negative intervention in response to the tendency to allow destiny to take over always consists of breaking destiny to bring about flexible situations in which mankind will have new opportunities to create. God does not send down to earth from the heavens a ready-made institution.

The role you have chosen for yourself in your work consists of explaining God's action—according to you, he operates uniquely through human beings.

Yes, but here again it is a retrospective view of things. On thinking of my life for this book, I said to myself, "I played this particular role." I didn't choose it for myself in advance. I continually groped my way along, knowing that I could not let go of either my analysis of the world or the biblical truth, and knowing I couldn't make the synthesis of them. I really had to operate in both fields at the same time, and in doing so I understood the historical role of God. He never ceases to give us opportunities. In a history that tends to repeat itself, the biblical God appears as one who makes the new break through by providing an opportunity to change established situations.

According to you, history has become a bit more flexible in the past several years; possibilities appear more numerous to you than they did twenty years ago. Do you see in this, retrospectively, an intervention by God? But you also speak fairly often of the silence he presently observes. How do you reconcile all this?

The present period, I maintain, seems to be a period in which God is silent, but something amazing is taking place: more and more people, without intervening in history on the level I would like to see, and contrary to all expectations, are recognizing the truth of God in Jesus Christ. The decline of the western church seems fortunate to me in the sense that those who drift away from the church never really belonged to it. There was a crisis in this church. But it was a crisis dating back to the eighteenth century whose results appeared only abruptly in the nineteen-fifties. And it had to happen to purify the situation: now the truth of God can again be proclaimed, free from political and social compromises, from class distinctions, and above all, from the illegitimate use of Christianity. By God's grace, it is no longer *useful* to be a Christian or to make reference to the church and the Bible.

And in those who remain I observe a really remarkable deepening of faith. In my youthful days, such a change was more than I could hope for. Isn't it miraculous that there are some extraordinarily committed Christians in Russia, and that more and more scientists, absolutely not Christians, are becoming acquainted with the God-hypothesis? These factors oblige me to believe that the world determined by Technique is not entirely closed. Every time I see one of these openings, I say to myself: "Man is responding to God, even though this God be silent!"

With this foundation, can you be read and really understood by people who do not share your faith?

It is certain that one cannot understand fully my books on sociology except through an affirmation of faith. Inversely, one cannot analyze the content of my books on theology without considering them written for this world. For both are written in the eschatological light of final salvation and reconciliation. I don't believe that this world and the men who live in it are lost, because the Bible constantly affirms that men are promised salvation and that the world is promised to enter into the heavenly Jerusalem. The end of history is a positive end.

You don't believe in a small remnant?

No. On the contrary, I have the firm conviction that salvation is universal because the love of God encompasses all. As I see it, this proposition is theologically indisputable: If God is God and if God is love, nothing is outside of the love of God. A place like hell is thus inconceivable. The worst of human beings is still necessarily in the love of God.

The difference between the Christian and the non-Christian is not one of salvation. For me, salvation is given by grace to everyone. Christians are simply those charged by God with a special mission. As I said a few moments ago, God does not act directly and immediately in history, but through the agency of those he calls to his service. This is what it means to be a Christian, not working at your own little salvation, but changing human history. And this is not necessarily done through political action. It can also be done through the preaching of the word of God.

Without the requirement of special preparation?

Without having anything other than the knowledge that God loves us. Even if our hearts cannot perceive God, we have been able to strive as Christians to serve by proclaiming the word of God as it is given in the Bible and by serving others. It is an economic and social service, of course, but it is even more a help in the face of anguish and the fear of death; we remind people that there is a God present and that all they need to do is stand up to be free.

The Christian's role thus seems to you more tied to hope than to faith?

Quite right. Faith is the certainty that if God tells us, "I have chosen you," it is true. It doesn't guarantee my salvation, but it assures me that God has truly chosen me for his service. When Elijah withdrew to the desert, saying, "Everyone has betrayed me, I am all alone. Am I sure after all that God has chosen me?" he received his answer. God confirmed to him that he really had chosen him.

Isn't there lacking in your work a book that would describe in detail the meaning of the dual progression that inspires it?

First, I am in the process of giving that description here, furnishing a key that I have never yet given. Besides, I don't want to do the synthesis of my own work. It is not a program or a utopia that is at issue in this refusal, but the very conception I have of the irreconcilability of the revelation and the world. I refuse unification. I want to leave readers with these two observations, these two propositions, this contradiction, so that they will begin their history themselves. For I come back to this: the contradiction can only be resolved by moving on, by history. Each person in regard to this tension and this conflict has to elaborate his own history, invent his own life, not by chance, but having a certainty of the finality and meaning of it, and with a knowledge of the place where he must make this history. This is why I don't want to give a synthesis of my work, or even less, as I said before, give a program or try to make disciples or found a school of thought. The reader must work and proceed alone: the synthesis he will then make will be the product and the means of his own history.

I am happy only when I receive articles or even books by young people who, having used what I wrote as a foundation, go beyond or do something entirely different. They are not beloved disciples who repeat what I said. They have understood that they have to invent. And there are those—it is a very satisfying experience —who discover new things I have never thought of.

I also on occasion find myself in the presence of young Christians or young theologians who enthusiastically embrace everything I have written. I am then much more reticent. I do not at all encourage theological enthusiasm any more than I encourage someone to blindly follow a political or social leader.

14.

Being Torn

MADELEINE GARRIGOU-LAGRANGE: *Now is a good time to summarize. But before we do that, I would like for you to tell about the great moments in your life, the key moments.*

JACQUES ELLUL: In my youth, there were three. There was my discovery of poverty, of which I have already spoken. I remember that night of panic in 1929. My father was out of work and there was no more money in the house. At that moment, I passed from the stage of childhood to that of adulthood.

The second key moment was obviously my conversion—a very spectacular conversion, and I said I would not talk about it. I could give a historical account of

215

this complete about-face; in fact, I have already done it, and it will be published after my death. At any rate, one of my books is *The Judgment of Jonah,* because this sudden conversion was followed, on the spiritual level, by a hopeless attempt to escape that lasted for years.

Years of faith and refusal?

That's right—an intellectual incapacity to live according to what the Bible told me, an incapacity to start on the path God opened before me and in the service he asked of me.

The third great moment was meeting my wife, who also had made a spiritual journey. She was raised as a Catholic, and she broke abruptly with Christianity after an unfortunate response from a priest who was incapable of understanding doubt. At that point she began to question everything.

When I met her, she was very Nietzschean; she admired *Nourritures Terrestres,*[1] and she rebelled violently against everything Christian. And when I say that I never converted anyone, perhaps I did, however, have a role in my wife's conversion. She encountered the Bible and she became a Christian, maybe not through my influence, I don't really know. It was she who helped me take the step that allowed me to stop fleeing as I had done for years in the face of God's revelation. That was the third great moment of my life,

---

1. Title of a volume of poetry by André Gide meaning "Earthly Sustenance"; the poems have a hedonistic, antireligious character. —TRANS.

a humanly decisive moment that was equally decisive on the spiritual level. Let us say that between the ages of sixteen and twenty-four, these are the three disrupting events in my life.

It is striking that you don't include your encounter with Marxism. Is it that you tie it to your encounter with poverty?

Of course, but I am trying to give you the major elements of an existential nature. Marx was for me an intellectual awakening. Caught as I was in this incomprehensible world of poverty, he gave me some ideas that enabled me to explain. Nothing more. And I can say that the existential void I found in Marx was filled by Christianity. I know that from a Marxist point of view this could be labeled a bourgeois concern, but it in fact reveals the extreme weakness and poverty of Marxism.

Would you say that you have become who you are through moments of intuition, through lightning revelations followed by a process of thought and development, and that you work in this way, in two modes?

That's fairly accurate. I have a nature that is, shall we say, poetic in the etymological sense of the word. And it is true that I have sudden intuitions that I then think over and reason out.

Do you ever fight these intuitions?

I try to escape them, but I can't escape the fact that something has taken place. When I was converted, I did all I could to fight God, yet I couldn't erase from my life those three or four hours I had lived. They were the fruit of neither illusion nor circumstances. It was no use, I really had experienced them.

That would be an example of a progressive evolution in your thought.

No, because I was faced with some hard questions. And I only evolve—it's a fact—by intuition or by the impact of such questions. In reality, I have the impression of living contrary to my temperament. By nature I would be incredibly lazy, I would like to let myself go and enjoy things and nature, but I have been led to become a man who is too busy, too organized, and too overworked.

In the same way, I don't feel I am by temperament a man in search of tragedies, and I have constantly had to fight tragedies. They came from the outside; I didn't look for them. I didn't want to be fired in 1940; I was, and it was a singular shock.

And there was this other tragedy when we lost one of our sons. But I prefer not to talk about it.

All my life there have been these disruptions that I was forced to face. It was impossible for me to run away. I will say that one thing about them did fit in with my temperament: I have never liked to run away. To be honest, I don't believe I have ever backed away or fled from any circumstance.

You said a few minutes ago, regarding God, "I fled."

From God, yes, it's true. It seemed impossible for me to continue the dialogue with him. But these questions that I was faced with, no, I never backed away from them or from danger, either.

Would you define yourself as a utopian, or a realist? Or as a man who, trying to walk on both legs, has one foot in realism and one foot in utopianism?

I seriously believe I am not at all a utopian; I have already said how much all utopias irritate me, both for their lack of realism and for their authoritarianism.

One may wonder if you don't give the appearance of being a utopian, or if you don't take yourself for a "prophet"—I put the word in quotation marks. Haven't you said that your books published twenty or thirty years ago seem more realistic today than at the time you wrote them? Were you a realist before everyone else?

That's it, quite simply, and nothing to do with prophecy. I see reality, and in this reality I know how to distinguish the dominant facts and tendencies for the future. And then I draw conclusions, whereas most of my colleagues are fixated on the biggest current phenomenon (which is doomed to fall into decline), or else they are bogged down in the past. But when I make these evaluations, they are not scientific, they are not scientific predictions. That type of evaluation usually turns out to be in error.

I will without restriction label myself a realist, even

in the domain of faith. Certain theology books bore me immeasurably, those that are intellectual dissertations. All these treatises on the nature of God do not interest me in the least. What is important to me is that which belongs to the ethical domain and the existential domain, in other words, what is close to life, to reality. I have never been able to finish reading a gnostic work. They bore me terribly. They talk of so-called mysteries that I will never experience. There is no wisdom in that. I am just as bored by the great utopians of the nineteenth century. They bore me because I don't see that their utopias have a chance to succeed or that they help in living. It doesn't interest me either to say: "In the year 2050, society will be like this or like that." What does interest me is to know what it will be like ten years from now. I always take as realistic as possible a perspective to make an analysis. Making predictions for thirty years from now is easy. None of us will be left to see if the predictions were correct. You can predict anything.

Aren't you a realist who expects things that others consider impossible? Don't your activities reflect the hope or even the belief that another kind of society is possible? And aren't what you call your failures tied to the fact that your undertakings are very daring, to say the least?

As I already said in regard to anarchy, I am not a utopian inasmuch as I don't believe it is possible to achieve an anarchist or a totally self-governing society. But since I believe that a society is alive only when contradicting factors interact, my action does not aim at producing a different kind of society but to introduce into the society we live in, on a very real and concrete level, the indispensable factors that will cause things to evolve, that will maintain some flexibility in the institutions and maintain an opportunity for human beings to exercise liberty. That is my aim above all else: that each person discover that he can play his own hand. To accomplish this, we cannot wait for a global transformation of society, or urge people to join totalitarian movements, or make them live under the illusion that "our day will come, of course on the condition that we accept the sacrifice of two or three generations." Only the present interests me with its predictable developments. And in this present, I am a realist, for I always try to calculate the possibilities, the efficacity, the value of an action, without much hope that it will produce something big but with the certainty that, in doing this, I am forcing society to evolve differently than its own logic would.

You are shaking it up.

If I can! But society is too big a word. I am content with one social setting, one situation, one institution. More than this would be unrealistic.

And you see yourself thus playing the role God asks of Christians in history, the role of a sort of troublemaker?

Yes, troublemakers, or creators of uncertainty. Contrary to the general view of the Christian as a messenger of certainty, I believe we ought to be messengers of uncertainty, troublemakers, since we are witnesses and thus agents (ambassadors, says Paul) of a dimension incompatible with society. Every time the social body succeeds in reducing this truth, classifying it, imprisoning it, it reappears abounding, contradicting, in another place. It prevents society from locking itself into a finished system.

Therefore you are not at all a man of order.

Here again I am in complete contradiction with myself. By preference I am a man of order. I like everything to unfold without a hitch, for my day's schedule to be precisely planned. I am unhappy in disorder. And I was called to provoke disorder and conflicts everywhere I am. It is certainly not by preference or by choice. I am very uncomfortable in the disorder produced by the destruction of societies. But I cannot tolerate external and formal order. I firmly believe in the creation of a continually renewed order. Equilibrium is not a static thing, but an imbalance constantly restored to order. This is not an original idea any more, but I have seen it to be true in my experience, namely, that order is born from disorder, and imbalances alone are creative. Freedom, too, is never established once and for all; it has to constantly be reconquered, lost, and gambled for again. So I would not say that I am a man of order but rather a man who believes in the necessity of a constantly renewed action.

A man who doesn't want history to fall asleep.

Or society to become standardized. For example, I cannot accept a communist society or a technical society because they are totally lacking in flexibiliy, and there is no play in their mechanism.

In your eyes, the supreme evil is ossification, fixation?

Not only the supreme evil, but *the* evil: it is paralysis, entropy, repetition, identicalness, unity, duplication.

Determinism, too?

Certainly. I work furiously to point out determinisms, both on the historical and sociological levels, in order to act as a doctor who gives a diagnosis: here is where we are. If we do nothing, here is how society will probably evolve. We must, then, intervene.

Aren't you tempted to dramatize the situation so that the points of breakdown can be seen more clearly?

I have changed a lot in this area. In my early writing, in *The Technological Society,* for example, I dramatized in order to back people into a corner, because I had the conviction that human beings are so negligent, so lazy, that if they are not driven to defend themselves, they will do everything possible to avoid commitment. Marx, too, dramatized in order to make the working class react. And I believe that this remains quite true. As long as a way out still seems possible, people do nothing and allow things to happen.

I do not write in quite the same way now, because the incredibly frivolous and thoughtless world of my youth has given way to a general conviction in people that the situation is hopeless. People today are afraid. Thus I will not tell them, in regard to the atomic bomb: "It is appalling, we will all be blown away." I think, on the contrary, that I should say: "There are ninety-nine chances in a hundred that it will never explode." I dramatize much less than thirty years ago because the adults of this age and, even more so the young people, are without hope.

I have another question that concerns you more personally. In 1936 you and your friend Charbonneau wrote a personalist manifesto in which one finds, thirty years in advance, some of the emphases of the 1968 demonstrators. And all your life you have looked for and proposed revolutionary disruptions. But you seem to live as a bourgeois in your beautiful home, surrounded by trees, books, music, and comfort. Do you feel that all this is consistent?

It is true that the comforts of life I enjoy now could seem completely contradictory to a revolutionary position. But I don't think that the revolutionary attitude, as I have tried to describe it, requires an identification with the poorest people in society. Nevertheless I do believe that an asceticism is necessary. For me, it was an asceticism of work and of availability. Every time I felt an action was necessary, it was as difficult for me to commit myself totally as it would be to live with some kind of material deprivation. In fact, we experienced a great deprivation between 1940 and 1945, and we put up with it quite well.

That wasn't exactly my question. Your manifesto was very intransigent on any compromise with liberal society. For example, it rejected the possibility of money bearing interest. Was this just the strictness of youth or have you lived according to these principles?

Yes and no. It is certain that I have tried all my life to follow the rules I fixed for myself with respect to the source and the use of money or insurance. But it isn't always easy when circumstances place you in situations determined by your social class, contrary to your convictions. Still, my wife and I have always observed an extremely strict discipline in regard to money: never save, never have money stored up, live from month to month, spending what is necessary and giving away the remainder. I don't have a cent of money in savings.

In the same way—and this point was a test for us for a long time—we refused for nearly twenty years to receive reimbursements from the national health insurance. I paid into it, but since my income allowed me to pay for my doctor visits and medications, I felt it was improper to ask for the reimbursement from the national health insurance. Since then, I have lost in this vain combat; I have fallen into line. But I am not proud of it.

These are some small examples from real life that I give, not to impress people, but to prove that we have kept watch to assure that our practice be consistent with our goal of revolution and transformation. I have always tried to write exactly as I live and to live as I have written.

But one encounters many more difficulties than just that of money. For example, the difficulty of time. I am always tempted by *doing,* and my wife has quite rightly emphasized *being,* relationships, the other person. How should we live the time that is accorded us? It was not only a question of schedule and establishing a budget of my time, which was already hard enough. I have always had the impression that time in my life is torn—I would say torn between what I believe to be my vocation, and the demands of the faith. I will explain: I have always felt I have an intellectual vocation, which implies a certain activity, my writing and my commitments. But, in contrast, there are the implications of the revelation (revealing the God who is love): being with others, sharing with them, as opposed to the isolation of the intellectual; being available, being there when the other has need of me, regardless of my obligation elsewhere to complete a book. Now, if I am not available in this way, all I say and write about Christianity has no meaning or truth to it. But if I remain available, then I cannot work.

And the contradiction worsens, for as I produce a coherent, fairly structured and rigorous thought, I will inevitably have an influence, will dominate others. This is exactly the opposite of my understanding of the revelation: to serve; yet my becoming an intellectual authority puts others in a state of inferiority. Therefore, I am constantly being torn, I live in uncertainty. On the one hand I live with the regret of not having done all the work I could have, and on the other hand, I have a bad conscience for not having given myself entirely to others. I have not been able to follow the admirable example of *Seed Beneath the Snow*. [2]

So I am faced with the necessity of continually reassessing my use of time, questioning it. Never satisfied. This is where the "Forgive us our debts" of the Lord's Prayer takes on its full significance. I feel I have an immense debt toward God and humanity, a debt of love, that I will never repay. But please don't think this makes me unhappy. This bad conscience is not guilt in the psychological sense, because I experience it within the certainty of grace that covers all that. Nevertheless, in reality, it is difficult to sort it out.

Can you assess your influence?

With the Reformed Church, it's very simple: I had practically none. Not only did my great plan to make of it a revolutionary kind of force in opposition to technical society fail completely, but I irritated the Protestants to the point that they consider me unclassifiable, a confirmed critic and a radical. With the exception of my friends, of course, I think I have had no influence in the Reformed Church. I have much more in some Catholic or nonbeliever circles.

As for influence on my students, it is difficult to evaluate. I have the *impression* that I had good contact with them. I didn't have to wait for Bourdieu to tell me how

---

2. Title of a novel by Italian left-wing writer Ignazio Silone, 1940.—TRANS.

much the college lecture could be illusory and false in the system of relations, and how much it could engender conformity even when it aimed at being nonconformist. I came to this realization very early. That is why I can only speak of an impression in my relations with students. All the same, I have kept on very friendly terms with some of them, though I haven't seen them for twenty or twenty-five years. They tell me—is it out of kindness?—that they found something in my teaching. At any rate, they gave me more than I felt I gave them. They played a very important role; each time I think and I write, their questions are stimulating me, and I am addressing them.

Do your students read your books?

I believe many students read my books. But when they know me well, some of them tell me I am very cold and that contact with me is very difficult. Others keep their distance from this important man who writes books and makes television appearances and is not just a professor. I am reminded of a former student who, years later, told me bluntly that he had never tried to approach me so as not to look as though he were seeking favors.

Aren't you better known in other countries and on other continents?

Of course. I can even say that *The Technological Society* was taken seriously in France only after the Americans became enthusiastic about it.

Are your foreign readers more numerous than those in France?

By far. Imagine that *The Technological Society* had a printing of around a hundred thousand copies in the United States. It was published there in 1962, twelve years after I wrote it. And it happens that I had very precisely described what the American society would become in the sixties. In France, they could not take me seriously. They told me: "You can easily see that it isn't happening the way you described it." Obviously, but it was indeed *going* to happen like that. When my book was published in the United States, it fit in exactly with the situation and, as no one had yet made this analysis, people saw in it the book that really explained to them what they had been experiencing for several years. That is why it was a success.

A success on the level of the analysis alone or on the level of action as well?

Some American friends tell me: "Your book on Technique has become the basic textbook for the subject of sociology in many universities. A great many theses are being done on your works." In fact, right now, doctoral theses on my works are cropping up in various places all over the world. Also, young people's groups have used the book as a tool for analyzing society and provoking change in it.

When the revolts exploded on the campuses between 1964 and 1968, I had a lot of correspondence.

Are your sociology books more widely read in the United States than your theology books?

No. The theology books followed. All were immediately published there, and they are given a wide distribution.

Even those that you have had a hard time publishing in France?

Some were first published in the United States. For example, *The Ethics of Freedom*, which I finished in 1972, and of which the third volume has not yet been published in France, came out immediately in 1973 in the United States as one enormous volume.

Now that the momentum has slowed down on the campuses, do your analyses and your assertions interest Americans as much as before?

Yes, because they have grasped the coherence of what I write. Many researchers and groups apply my method to new problems. A group of professors belonging to different universities has even published a book of several essays on my works, and they asked me to contribute a detailed study of the dialectic; this was for the academic audience.

Do you think that Americans are more interested in your analyses than the French because they are closer to a pre-revolutionary situation?

I don't think they are in a prerevolutionary situation in

the classical sense, but they are becoming more and more conscious of the impossibility of continuing with the technocapitalist thrust. Americans have one outstanding quality that we do not have in France (and which is even more lacking in Russia), that of being able to recognize their errors, to accept this realization, and to modify, rectify, or even cancel. They will accept doing the opposite of what was believed correct thirty years before. They have a flexibility and a capacity to start over that expresses honesty, but it also insures success. If they see that modern Technique is really a mistake in itself, they are capable of questioning it all. In France, however much everyone agrees that it is disastrous to build huge housing developments or supertankers, we continue to do it.

What has really counted for you in your life?

I have already told you: my conversion, meeting my wife, and friendships. I have been a man of friendships, and this has enormously counted in my life. The rest—career, honors, titles—has never interested me. But when I think back on my life, as you ask me to do, I find that I have been incredibly happy, and I feel I have been amazingly protected. To have gone through without a hitch what I went through from 1940 to 1945 is extraordinary. Never to have been sick is a tremendous gift. I see the sickness and misfortune that strike around me and I look at my life—it is true that it was a hard life; it started from nothing and was constantly at the breaking point, but I have always lived my life in happiness.

Do you feel you have accomplished the essential of what you wanted to do? Are you the man you wanted to become?

I would not wish another life. I don't regret anything I *didn't* have; I don't regret any imaginary joys; from time to time I say to myself: "It is certain now that I will never see Mexico, I will make no more overseas voyages. There are works of art I would have liked to encounter, and I will never see them." Just a small regret. But I profoundly regret the missed encounters, the word I should have said to someone who came to see me and died soon after without having heard what he came seeking. There are a lot of things I repent of. But it is an affair between God and me. As for the general direction of my life, the great choices, if I had to start over I would start over the same way. I don't even miss the sea. My father really was right. I had a much more exciting life than if I had been commander of some oil tanker.

And you wouldn't like to have done some things differently?

In some concrete circumstances, yes. "For I do not do the good I want, but the evil I do not want is what I do." I didn't accomplish all I would have liked to accomplish, my actions didn't have the results that I hoped for, that is certain. It didn't click. I was mistaken in my hope of triggering the beginning of a transformation of society.

Do you think you were speaking to deaf ears?

I don't pass judgments. I said what I thought, and it was not heard. I probably said it badly. But much more important, I may have had the opportunity at times to bear witness to Jesus Christ. Perhaps through my words or my writing, someone met this savior, the only one, the unique one, beside whom all human projects are childishness; then, if this has happened, I will be fulfilled, and for that, glory to God alone.

Biographical Notes

Academic: *License* in law, 1931. *License* in literature, 1932. *Doctorat* in law, 1936.

Taught at Montpellier and Strasbourg, 1937–1940.

Fired by the Vichy government, 1940.

Agrégé (graduate competitive exam for professors) by the School of Law, 1943.

Professor at the School of Law at Bordeaux, 1944.

Professor at the Institute of Political Studies, 1947.

Retired, 1980.

Activities: Resistance, 1940–1944.

Assistant to the mayor of Bordeaux, 1944–1946.

Regional secretary of the *Mouvement de Libération nationale* (National Liberation Movement), 1944–1946.

Member of the special committees of the *Conseil oecuménique des Eglises* (Ecumenical Council of Churches), 1947–1951.

Member of the national synod of the Reformed Church of France until 1970.

Member of the national council of the Reformed Church, 1951–1970.

Various social service activities in specialized prevention and in defense of the environment.

Editor of the journal *Foi et Vie.*

Literary: 36 books published to date, and translations in 12 foreign languages.

210 articles in journals and magazines.

Honors: *Doctorat honoris causa* from the universities of Amsterdam and Aberdeen.

Officer of the Legion of Honor.

Officer of the Order of Merit.

High officer of the academic *Palmes.*

Literary Awards: History prize of the Académie Française, 1942.

European prize for essay, Louis Veillon award, 1975.

Bibliography

Apocalypse: The Book of Revelation. Trans. George W. Schreiner. New York: Seabury, 1977. *L'Apocalypse, architecture en mouvement.* Paris: Desclée de Brouwer, 1975.

Autopsy of Revolution. Trans. Patricia Wolf. New York: Knopf, 1971. *Autopsie de la Révolution.* Paris: Calmann-Lévy, 1969.

Betrayal of the West. Trans. Matthew J. O'Connel. New York: Seabury, 1978. *Trahison de l'Occident.* Paris: Calmann-Lévy, 1975.

A Critique of the New Commonplaces. Trans. Helen Weaver. New York: Knopf, 1968. *Exégèse des nouveaux lieuxs communs.* Paris: Calmann-Lévy, 1966.

The Ethics of Freedom. Trans. G. W. Bromiley. Grand Rapids, Mich.: Eerdmans, 1976. *L'éthique de la liberté.* 3 vols. Geneva: Labor et Fides, 1973–.

False Presence of the Kingdom. Trans. C. Edward Hopkin. New York: Seabury, 1972. *Fausse présence au monde moderne.* Paris: E.K.F., 1964.

Hope in Time of Abandonment. Trans. C. Edward Hopkin. New York: Seabury, 1973. *L'espérance oubliée.* Paris: Gallimard, 1977.

The Judgment of Jonah. Trans. G. W. Bromiley. Grand Rapids, Mich.: Eerdmans, 1971. *Le livre de Jonas.* Paris: Cahiers Bibliques de Foi et Vie, 1952.

The Meaning of the City. Trans. Dennis Pardee. Grand Rapids, Mich.: Eerdmans, 1970. *Sans feu ni lieu.* Paris: Gallimard, 1975.

The New Demons. Trans. C. Edward Hopkin. New York: Seabury, 1975. *Les nouveaux possédés.* Paris: Fayard, 1973.

The Political Illusion. Trans. Konrad Keller. New York: Knopf, 1967. *L'illusion politique.* Paris: R. Laffont, 1965.

The Politics of God and the Politics of Man. Trans. G. W. Bromiley. Grand Rapids, Mich.: Eerdmans, 1972. *Politique de Dieu, politiques des hommes.* Paris: Editions Universitaires, 1966.

Prayer and Modern Man. Trans. C. Edward Hopkin. New York: Seabury, 1970. *L'impossible prière.* Paris: Le Centurion, 1971.

The Presence of the Kingdom. Trans. Olive Wyon. Philadelphia: Westminster, 1951; New York: Seabury, 1967. *Présence au monde moderne.* Geneva: Roulet, 1948.

Propaganda: the Formation of Men's Attitudes. Trans. Konrad Kellen and Jean Lerner. New York: Knopf, 1965. *Propagandes.* Paris: Armand Colin, 1962.

The Technological Society. Rev. Amer. ed. Trans. John Wilkinson. New York: Knopf, 1964. *La technique ou l'enjeu du siècle*. Paris: Armand Colin, 1954.

The Technological System. New York: Seabury, 1980. *Le système technicien*. Paris: Calmann-Lévy, 1977.

The Theological Foundation of Law. Trans. Marguerite Wieser. Garden City, N.Y.: Doubleday, 1960; New York: Seabury, 1969. *Le fondement théologique du droit*. Neufchâtel and Paris: Delachaux et Niestlé, 1946.

To Will and to Do: An Ethical Research for Christians. Trans. C. Edward Hopkin. Philadelphia: Pilgrim, 1969. *Le vouloir et le faire: Récherches éthiques pour les chrétiens*. Geneva: Labor et Fides, 1964.

Violence: Reflections from a Christian Perspective. Trans. Cecelia Gaul Kings. New York: Seabury, 1969. *Contre les violents*. Paris: Le Centurion, 1972.

WORKS NOT AVAILABLE IN ENGLISH

De la révolution aux révoltes. Paris: Calmann-Lévy, 1972.

L'Empire du non-sens. Paris: P.U.F., 1980.

Essai sur le recrutement de l'armée française aux XVIe–XVIIe siècles. Mémoires de l'Académie des sciences morales, 1941.

Etude sur l'évolution et la nature juridique du Mancipium. Thèse pour le doctorat. Bordeaux: Delmas, 1936.

La foi au prix de doute. Paris: Hachette, 1980.

Histoire de la propagande. Paris: P.U.F., 1967; 2nd ed., 1976.

Histoire des institutions. Paris: Presses Universitaires de France. Vol. 1/2: *L'Antiquité*, 1951–52, rev. ed. 1972; Vol. 3: *Le moyen age*, 1953, rev. ed. 1975–80; Vol 4: *XVIe–XVIIIe siècles*, 1956, rev. 1976; Vol 5: *XIXe siècle*, 1957, rev. 1979.

L'homme et l'argent. Neufchâtel and Paris: Delachaux, 1953; Re-edited by P.B.U., 1979.

L'idéologie marxiste chrétienne, Paris: Le Centurion, 1979.

Introduction à l'histoire de la discipline des Eglises Réformées. Bordeaux: the author, 1943.

Jeunesse délinquante, with Yves Charrier. Paris: Mercure de France, 1971.

La Parole humiliée. Paris: Le Seuil, 1981.

Métamorphose du bourgeois. Paris: Calmann-Lévy, 1967.

Index

237

World War II
Gide, André, 216 n
Giono, Jean, 137
Girls, in juvenile delinquent club, 122
God, 16, 58, 59, 67–83 *passim*, 91–93, 140, 213; and creation, 140–41, 142; and dialectical process, 203, 204, 206–11; and Ellul's conversion, 14, 216, 218–19; kingdom of, 59, 76, 88–89, 91, 196; as liberator, 80, 81, 183–84; love of, 24, 28, 76–77, 78, 92, 134, 141, 142, 212
Goethe, J. W. von, 15
Grace, 76, 77, 79, 80, 204, 227
"Great workers' movement," 52
Groups, 190–91; juvenile delinquent, 120, 121–27, 132, 137; political, 37, 38–39, 43–44; professional, 63–66, 84–85

Happiness, 7, 8, 231
Hegel, G. W. F., 60
Hell, 76
History, 91–93, 160, 179, 184–86, 211, 212; and dialectical process, 197, 202–3, 205, 207, 208–10; Roman law and, 20–21, 22, 159–60, 174
History of Institutions, 184–85, 186
Hitler, Adolf, 44
Holloway, James, x
Holy Spirit, 94
Homosexuality, 28–29
Honor, 5, 6, 7, 8
Hope, 95, 224
Hope in Time of Abandonment, 183
Human nature, 205–6
Hutchins, Robert, *vii*
Huxley, Aldous, *vii*

Individual action, 197, 198, 199–200
Institute of Political Studies, 160, 169
Institutes, 16

Institutions, 184–86
Intellectual poverty, of juvenile delinquents, 120
Intellectual solitude, 193–94
Interventions, God's, 209, 210
Introducing Jacques Ellul, x
Intuitions, 217–18

Jeremiah, *xi*
Jesus Christ, 2, 3, 24, 25, 31, 64, 75, 76, 88–89, 91–92, 96–97, 134, 184, 210, 233
Jews, 95
Jèze strike, 34
Jonah (*Judgment of Jonah*), 175, 216
Justice, 76, 77, 181, 182
Juvenile delinquents, 75, 117–38

Kairos, 209
Kapital, 4, 11
Kierkegaard, Søren, 17, 59, 81
Kingdom of God, 59, 76, 88–89, 91, 196

Lacanau, 147, 150–51
Landes forest, 143, 156
Law, 19–22, 179–80, 184–85; and Aquitaine issue, 149; Ellul's father and, 19–20, 48; and juvenile delinquents, 117; Roman, 20–22, 45, 159–60, 174; teaching of, 21, 50, 159–60
Lévy, Bernard Henry, 36 n, 207
Liberal Christians, *xiii*, 78
Liberty, 64, 80–81, 183–84, 195, 209, 222
Love: and creation, 141, 142; God's, 24, 28, 76–77, 78, 92, 134, 141, 142, 212
Luther, Martin, 93, 175

Making of a Counter Culture, *viii*
Mancipium, 185–86
Marc, Alexandre, 35
Marcuse, Herbert, *viii*, 130
Marx, Karl, 2, 3, 11–19 *passim*, 40,